The BIG OKLAHOMA Reproducible Activity Book!

BY CAROLE MARSH

This activity book has material which correlates with Oklahoma's Priority Academic Student Skills.

At every opportunity, we have tried to relate information to the History and Social Science, English, Science, Math, Civics, Economics, and Computer Technology Oklahoma PASS directives.

For additional information, go to our website: **www.gallopade.com**

Published by
GALLOPADE™ INTERNATIONAL
800-536-2GET
www.gallopade.com

Gallopade is proud to be a member or supporter of these educational organizations and associations:

ASCD · ABA American Booksellers Association · Association of Partners for Public Lands · NCSS

Cover character illustrations © Dawn Hudson I Agency: Dreamstime.com

The Big Activity Book Team

Billie Walburn
Michael Marsh
Steven Saint-Laurent
Antoinette Miller
Michele Yother
Carole Marsh
Bob Longmeyer
William Nesbitt, Jr.

Lisa Stanley
Sherry Moss
Cecil Anderson
Vicki DeJoy
Chad Beard
Jackie Clayton
Terry Briggs
Karin Petersen

Kathy Zimmer Wanda Coats Cranston Davenport Jill Sanders

The Oklahoma Experience Series

The Oklahoma Experience! Paperback Book

My First Pocket Guide to Oklahoma!

The Big Oklahoma Reproducible Activity Book

The Oklahoma Coloring Book!

My First Book About Oklahoma!

Oklahoma Jeopardy: Answers and Questions About Our State

Oklahoma "Jography!": A Fun Run Through Our State

The Oklahoma Experience! Sticker Pack

The Oklahoma Experience! Poster/Map

Discover Oklahoma CD-ROM

Oklahoma "GEO" Bingo Game

Oklahoma "HISTO" Bingo Game

A Word From The Author

Oklahoma is a very special state. Almost everything about Oklahoma is interesting and fun! It has a remarkable history that helped create the great nation of America. Oklahoma enjoys an amazing geography of incredible beauty and fascination. The state's people are unique and have accomplished many great things.

This Activity Book is chockful of activities to entice you to learn more about Oklahoma. While completing mazes, dot-to-dots, word searches, coloring activities, word codes, and other fun-to-do activities, you'll learn about Oklahoma's history, geography, people, places, animals, legends, and more.

Whether you're sitting in a classroom, stuck inside on a rainy day, or—better yet—sitting in the back seat of a car touring the wonderful state of Oklahoma, my hope is that you have as much fun using this Activity Book as I did writing it.

Enjoy your Oklahoma Experience—it's the trip of a lifetime!!

Carole Marsh

Color Me!
Oklahoma
BROWN
Like the fur of the mighty buffalo
Brown
BLUE
Like the Oklahoma sky
Blue
YELLOW
Like corn as high as an elephant's eye
Yellow
RED
Like Redbud blossoms
Red
BLACK
Like black gold—oil
Black
PURPLE
Like the sky at twilight
Purple
GREEN
Like the Oklahoma grassy plains
Green
ORANGE
Like Oklahoma clay
Orange

Our State Bird!

Connect the dots to see Oklahoma's beautiful state bird, the Scissor-tailed Flycatcher.

When you are done, color the bird.

Write the bird's name in the space below.

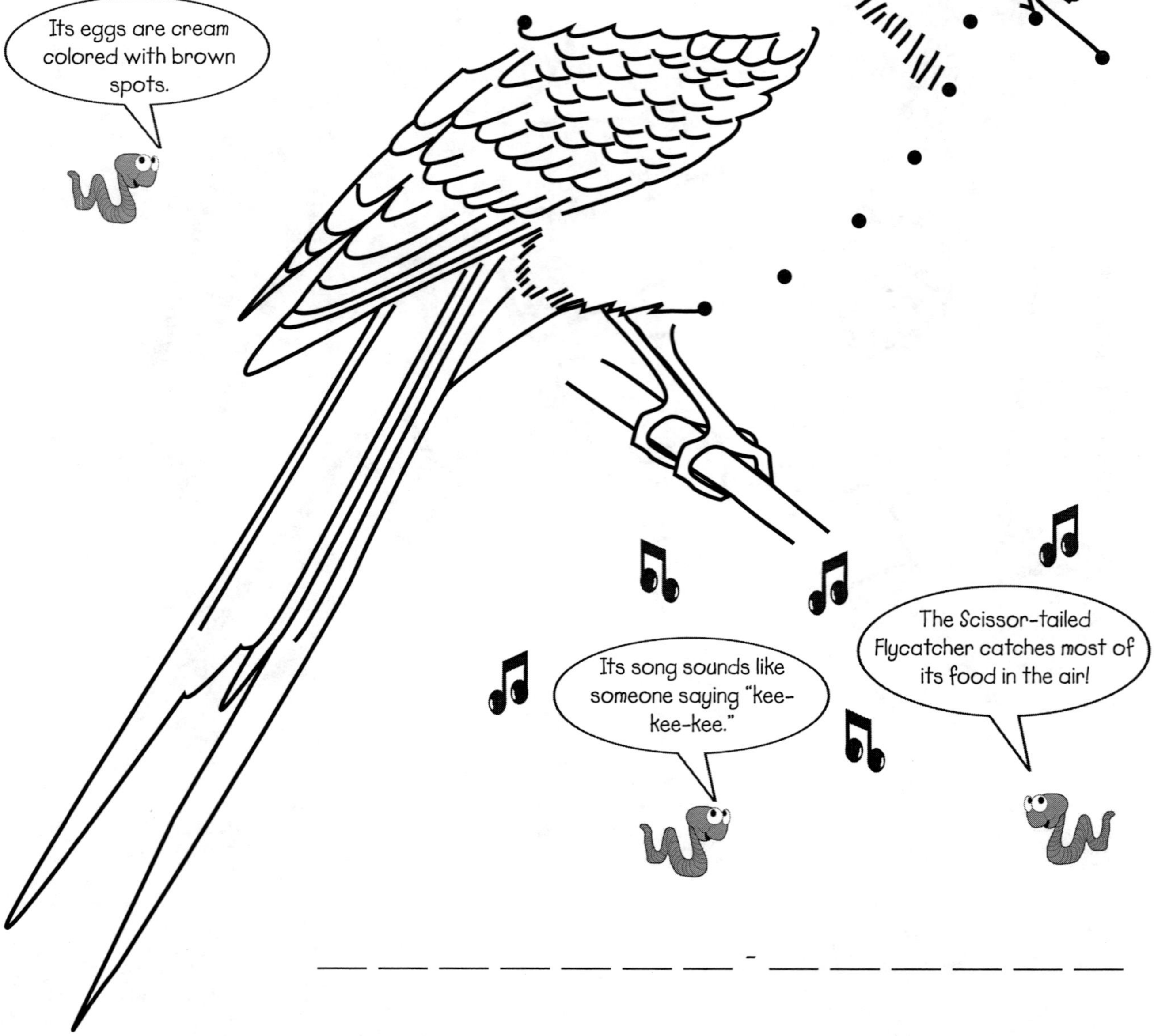

__ __ __ __ __ __ __ - __ __ __ __ __ __

__ __ __ __ __ __ __ __ __ __ __

Buffalo Soldiers!

In the 1800s, many African-Americans came to Oklahoma as farmers, settlers, cowboys, and gunfighters. They also fought in the Civil War. On July 17, 1863, African-American soldiers helped the Union win the Battle of Honey Springs (also known as the Battle of Elk Creek).

After the Civil War ended, Congress passed a bill that created two African-American infantry units at Fort Sill and Fort Gibson. They fought cattle thieves, bandits, and Mexican revolutionaries. They also fought in the Indian wars toward the end of the 1800s. These brave men were called "Buffalo Soldiers" by the Indians because of their tightly curled hair, which reminded the Indians of a buffalo's coat.

Answer the following questions:

1. Why did many African-Americans come to Oklahoma?

____

2. What battle did they help the Union win?

____

3. Where were the two infantry units that Congress created stationed?

____

4. What were these soldiers called by the Indians?

____

5. Why were they called that?

____

ANSWERS: (may vary slightly) 1.They were cowboys, settlers, farmers, and gunfighters. 2.the Battle of Honey Springs, or the Battle of Elk Creek 3.Fort Sill and Fort Gibson 4.Buffalo Soldiers 5.Their tightly curled hair reminded the Indians of a buffalo's coat.

All Around Oklahoma! Bubblegram!

Bubble up on your knowledge of Oklahoma's bordering states and bodies of water.

Fill in the bubblegram by using the clues below.

1. A state east of Oklahoma
2. A state south of Oklahoma
3. A state north of Oklahoma
4. A state northeast of Oklahoma
5. The capital of Oklahoma
6. A river in the eastern part of Oklahoma

1. ___ ___ ___ ___ (◯) ___ ___ ___
2. (◯) (◯) ___ ___ ___
3. ___ ___ ___ (◯) ___ (◯)
4. ___ ___ ___ ___ (◯) ___ ___ ___
5. (◯) ___ ___ ___ ___ ___ ___ ___   ___ ___ (◯) ___
6. ___ (◯) ___ (◯) ___ ___ ___ ___   ___ ___ ___ (◯) ___

Now unscramble the "bubble" letters to find out the mystery words!
Hint: What is Oklahoma's nickname?

The ___ ___ ___ ___ ___ ___   ___ ___ ___ ___ ___!

MYSTERY WORDS: Sooner State
ANSWERS: 1.Arkansas 2.Texas 3.Kansas 4.Missouri 5.Oklahoma City 6.Arkansas River

The Trail of Tears!

Some of the first Americans to settle in Oklahoma were Native Americans. In 1804, the United States federal government began moving Native Americans off their tribal lands east of the Mississippi River to the west. These Native Americans, the Cherokee, Choctaw, Creek, Seminole, and Chickasaw tribes, were known as the Five Civilized Tribes because they had adopted many of the colonists' customs. Many of them spoke English, dressed in European-style clothing, and even ran their own businesses and farms!

Soldiers were sent to Oklahoma to build forts to protect the Native Americans and to protect the region from the Spanish. The Native Americans established their own governments, school systems, and elected leaders. During the winter of 1838–1839, some 15,000 members of the Five Civilized Tribes of the East were forced to move to Oklahoma during a trip known as the Trail of Tears.

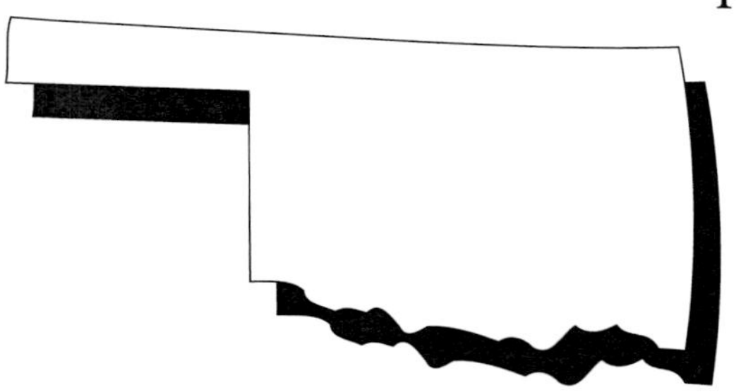

Answer the following questions.

1. Cross out the name of the tribe that was NOT a member of the Five Civilized Tribes.
   SEMINOLE IROQUOIS CHEROKEE CHOCTAW
2. In which direction were the Five Civilized Tribes forced to move? Circle the correct direction on the compass rose below:

3. What was the name given to the trip made by the Native Americans during the winter of 1838-1839?
   Trail of ________________
   (Hint: What comes out of your eyes when you cry?)
4. The U.S. federal government moved MORE or LESS (circle one) than 10,000 Native Americans during the winter of 1838-1839.

ANSWERS: 1.IROQUOIS 2.west 3.Tears 4.MORE

Oklahoma Wheel of Fortune, Indian Style!

The names of Oklahoma's many Native American tribes contain enough consonants to play . . . Wheel of Fortune!

See if you can figure out the Wheel of Fortune-style puzzles below! "Vanna" has given you some of the consonants in each word.

W _ C H _ T _

C _ D D _

Q _ _ P _ W

K _ _ W _   _ P _ C H _

P _ W N _ _

_ S _ G _

ANSWERS: WICHITA CADDO QUAPAW KIOWA APACHE PAWNEE OSAGE

Mounds Abound in Oklahoma!

People have lived in Oklahoma for MILLENNIA. Over thousands of years, several groups of NOMADIC people stopped their travels to settle in the area. From 500 BC to AD 1300, a group called the Mound Builders built large EARTHEN mounds to use as temples. EXCAVATION of these mounds has revealed pottery, textiles, and metalwork. Many of these ARTIFACTS are well crafted, and have helped scientists to learn more about the Mound Builders. After AD 1200, the Mound Builders were attacked by peoples from the western plains, and their culture DECLINED. They disappeared completely sometime after AD 1400. Nobody knows where they went!

See if you can figure out the meanings of these words from the story above.

1. millennia __________________________________

2. nomadic: __________________________________

3. earthen: __________________________________

4. excavation: __________________________________

5. artifacts: __________________________________

6. declined: __________________________________

Now check your answers in a dictionary. How close did you get to the real definitions?

In the Beginning... Came the Spanish

In 1541, Francisco Vásquez de Coronado came up from Mexico through western Oklahoma in search of gold and the fabled city of Quivira. He found Quivira, but no gold. However, he did make a bargain with the Native Americans there, and claimed the area for Spain.

Help Coronado find his way to Quivira!

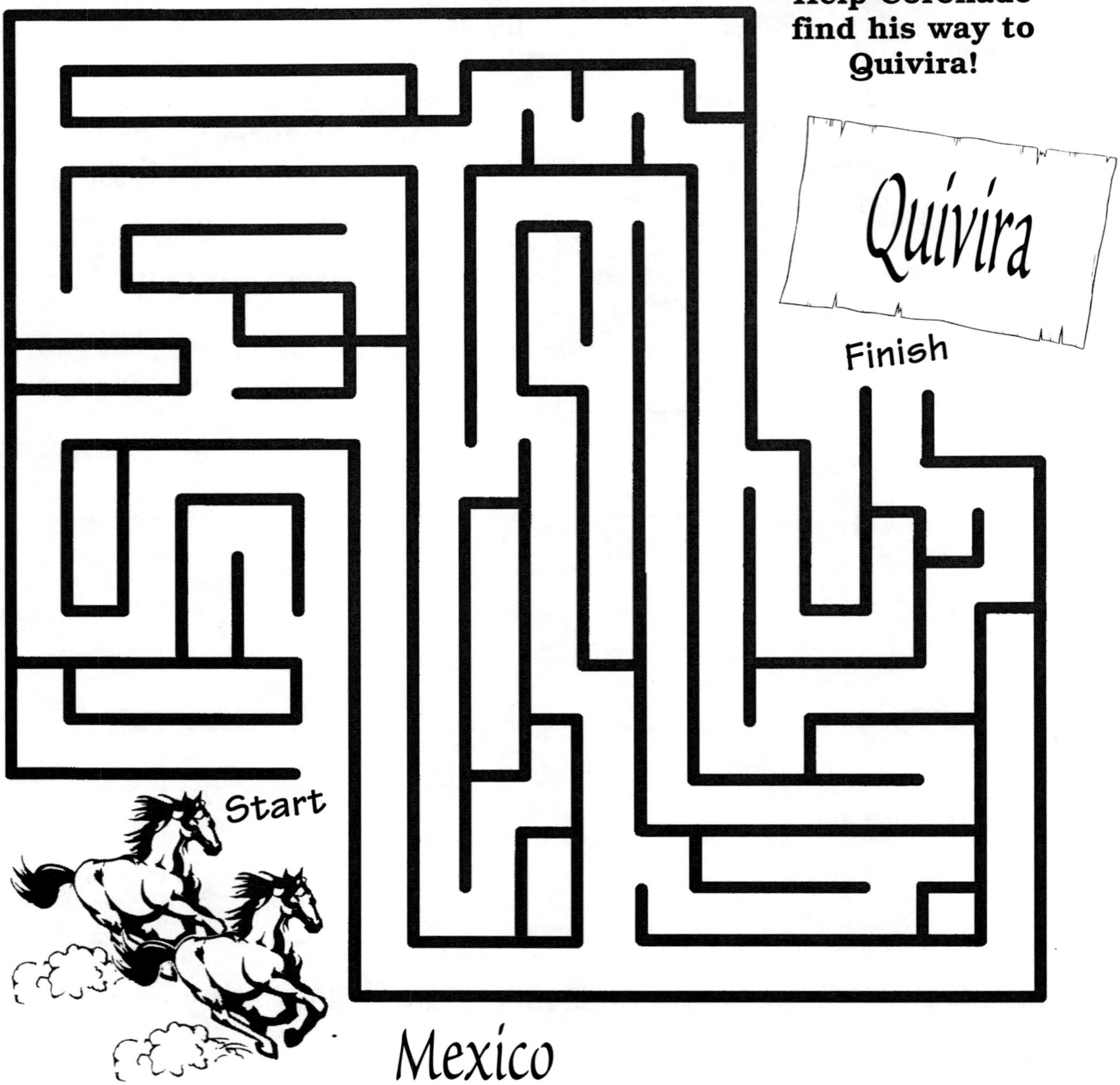

Sing Like an Oklahoma Bird Word Jumble!

Arrange the jumbled letters in the proper order for the names of birds found in Oklahoma.

SWALLOW
CARDINAL
QUAIL
SCISSOR-TAILED FLYCATCHER
MEADOWLARK
MOCKINGBIRD
PHEASANT
ROBIN
SPARROW
WILD TURKEY
CROW

N I D L A R A C ________

T E H P S A A N ________

N I B O R _____

K E A D W O M L A R __________

L I A Q U _____

S P R R W O A _______

W L L A S O W _______

D W I L K U T E R Y ____ ______

B R I D C K O G N I M ___________

W O R C ____

R A Y L E C F H T C S R I O S C S - L E D T I A

_______ ______-______ ___________

School Rules!

The first schools in Oklahoma were actually organized by the Five Civilized Tribes in the mid-1800s! The Native Americans moved there in the 1830s and opened schools for both boys and girls. Church groups from eastern states also founded schools in Oklahoma.

By the 1990s, Oklahoma had 29 public and 17 private colleges and universities. The University of Oklahoma was founded in 1890 in Norman, and in 1895 it had its first 100 students. Today, the University has over 20,000 students, and is the home of the Sam Noble Oklahoma Museum of Natural History!

Complete the names of these Oklahoma schools. Use the Word Bank to help you. Then, use the answers to solve the code at the bottom.

1. ___ ___ ___ ___(4) ___ ___(5) ___ ___ ___ ___ ___
   University in Tulsa

2. ___ ___ ___ ___ ___ ___ ___(6) ___ State
   University in Stillwater

3. ___(3) ___ ___ ___ ___ ___(2) ___ ___
   University in Enid

4. Oklahoma ___ ___(7) ___ ___ ___ ___ ___ University in Shawnee

5. University of Central Oklahoma in ___ ___(1) ___ ___ ___ ___

WORD BANK
Phillips
Edmond
Oral Roberts
Oklahoma
Baptist

The coded message tells you what all college students want.

___ ___ ___ ___ ___ ___ ___
1 2 3 4 5 6 7

ANSWERS: 1.Oral Roberts 2.Oklahoma 3.Phillips 4.Baptist 5.Edmond **MESSAGE:** diploma

Let's Get Physical!

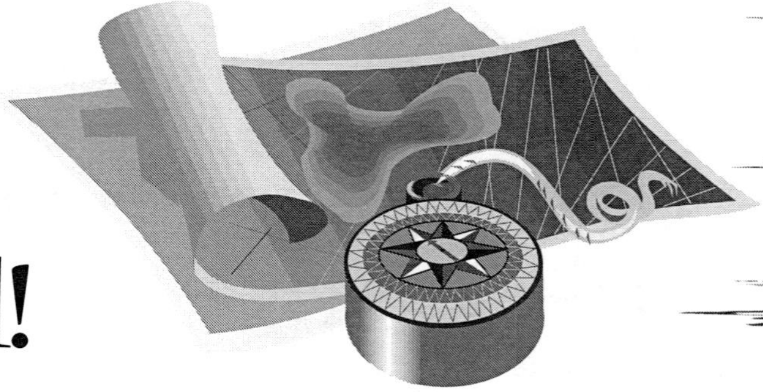

When we learn about the geography of Oklahoma, we use special words to describe it. These words describe the things that make each part of the state interesting. **See if you can match these geographical terms with their definitions!**

1. gorge
2. plain
3. tributary
4. port silt loam
5. mound
6. panhandle
7. reservoir
8. channel
9. mountain range
10. arroyo

A. a natural or artificial place where water is collected and stored for use

B. a deep, narrow passage between mountains

C. a pile or heap of earth

D. the bed of a stream, river, or other waterway

E. a gully where a small river or stream has dried up

F. a river or stream that flows into a larger body of water

G. dark reddish brown soil

H. a flat area of land with few variations

I. an extension of a territory or state that looks like a handle

J. a group of mountains

ANSWERS: 1.B 2.H 3.F 4.G 5.C 6.I 7.A 8.D 9.J 10.E

Oh! Say Can You See.... Oklahoma's State Flag!

Fourteen flags have flown over Oklahoma throughout its history. The current flag was adopted in 1925. It has a blue background, with a buckskin shield of an Osage warrior in the center. The shield is crossed by an olive branch and a peace pipe. The small tan crosses on the shield represent stars, which mean high ideals and endeavors. The word "Oklahoma" was added to the flag in 1941. **Color the state flag.**

Design your own Diamante on Oklahoma!

A *diamante* is a diamond-shaped poem on any subject.

You can write your very own diamante poem on Oklahoma by following the simple line by line directions below. Give it a try!

Line 1: Write the name of your state.

Line 2: Write the names of two animals native to your state.

Line 3: Write the names of three of your state's important cities.

Line 4: Write the names of four of your state's important industries or agricultural products.

Line 5: Write the name of your state bird.

Line 6: Write the names of two of your state's landforms.

Line 7: Write the word that completes this sentence: Oklahoma's nickname is the ________________ State

____

________________ ________________

________________ ________________ ________________

________________ ________________ ________________ ________________

________________ ________________ ________________

________________ ________________

____

Oklahoma, the Sooner State!

Match the name of each Oklahoma state symbol on the left with its picture.

State Bird

State Flower

State Tree

State Animal

State Fish

State Insect

Honeybee

Buffalo

Sand Bass (White Bass)

Scissor-tailed Flycatcher

Mistletoe

Redbud

History Mystery Tour!

Oklahoma is busting at the seams with history! Here are just a few of the many historical sites that you might visit. Try your hand at locating them on the map! **Draw the symbol for each site on the Oklahoma map below.**

❊ **The Harn Homestead:** William Fremont Harn built a farmhouse near Oklahoma City in 1904. Today, guides in period clothing give tours of the farmhouse, a stone and cedar barn, a 1900 working farm, and a gazebo.

✖ **The Cathedral of the Osage:** The Immaculate Conception Catholic Church in Pawhuska is also called the Cathedral of the Osage. It has 22 stained-glass windows! You can visit in June to see the traditional Osage ceremonial dances.

▲ **Fort Gibson Military Park:** Visitors to Muskogee can catch a glimpse of 19th century military life by touring the 12 restored or reconstructed buildings here. You can also see the U.S.S. *Batfish*, a World War II submarine, at the nearby Port of Muskogee.

✙ **Creek Council House Museum:** Okmulgee is the capital of the Creek (Muskogee) Nation. The original capitol building is now a museum where visitors can see exhibits of how the Creek Indians lived from the 16th through the 20th century. Several historical documents are on display.

Oklahoma Places to go! Things to do!

Use the Word Bank to help you complete the sentences below and learn about some of the exciting Oklahoma sites you can visit!

WORD BANK			
Will Rogers	Gilcrease	Allen	Tom Mix
Osage	Cherokee	Pecan	Great

1. You can see the world's largest collection of Western art and artifacts at the _ _ _ _ _ _ _ _ _ Museum in Tulsa.

2. Ride horses, go on hayrides, and eat a chuckwagon-style dinner at the _ _ _ _ _ Ranch.

3. Stop in Claremore to see the _ _ _ _ _ _ _ _ _ _ Memorial, dedicated to the great humorist.

4. Go to the _ _ _ _ _ Festival in Okmulgee and eat yourself silly on nutty delights!

5. Tahlequah is the home of the _ _ _ _ _ _ _ _ National Museum, and is also where the Trail of Tears ended.

6. See the life of the "King of Cowboys" when you visit the _ _ _ _ _ _ Museum.

7. You can see a replica of a fortified 1830s trading post when you go to the Museum of the _ _ _ _ _ Plains in Lawton.

8. Pawhuska is the capital of the _ _ _ _ _ Reservation, where several museums tell the story of the tribe's history.

ANSWERS: 1.Gilcrease 2.Allen 3.Will Rogers 4.Pecan 5.Cherokee 6.Tom Mix 7.Great 8.Osage

Outlaws and Lawmen!

During the second half of the 1800s, Oklahoma was a favorite hideout for many outlaws. Frank and Jesse James, the Younger Brothers, the Dalton Gang, Bill Doolin and his Wild Bunch, and Belle Starr took refuge there at one time or another. The outlaws would often rob banks, hold up trains, and commit various other crimes. There were also famous lawmen who chased the outlaws into Oklahoma, including the Three Guardsmen—Bill Tilghman, Heck Thomas, and Chris Madsen.

In the early 1900s, other famous criminals also hid in Oklahoma. These criminals included Pretty Boy Floyd, Bonnie and Clyde, and Machine-Gun Kelly. Many of them were also chased and captured while in Oklahoma.

Use information from the story above to complete the crossword.

1. Many famous criminals hid out in ______________. (ACROSS)
2. Another name for a criminal is _________________. (DOWN)
3. Bill Tilghman, Heck Thomas, and Chris Madsen were known as the Three ____________. (DOWN)
4. The men from #3 were also famous ____________. (ACROSS)
5. The outlaws in Oklahoma committed many ________. (ACROSS)

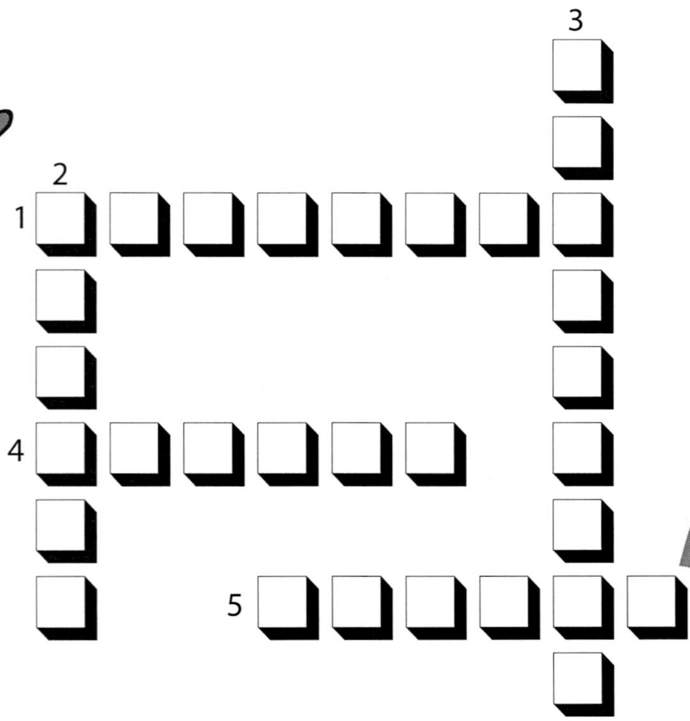

ANSWERS: 1. Oklahoma 2.outlaw 3.Guardsmen 4.lawmen 5.crimes

Oklahoma Rules!

Use the code to complete the sentences.

A	B	C	D	E	F	G	H	I	J	K	L	M	N	O	P	Q	R	S	T
1	2	3	4	5	6	7	8	9	10	11	12	13	14	15	16	17	18	19	20

U	V	W	X	Y	Z
21	22	23	24	25	26

1. State rules are called ___ ___ ___ ___.
   12 1 23 19

2. Laws are made in our state ___ ___ ___ ___ ___ ___ ___.
   3 1 16 9 20 15 12

3. The leader of our state is the ___ ___ ___ ___ ___ ___ ___ ___.
   7 15 22 5 18 14 15 18

4. We live in the state of ___ ___ ___ ___ ___ ___ ___ ___ .
   15 11 12 1 8 15 13 1

5. The capital of our state is

   ___ ___ ___ ___ ___ ___ ___ ___ ___ ___ ___ ___ .
   15 11 12 1 8 15 13 1 3 9 20 25

O K L A H O M A

ANSWERS: 1.laws 2.capitol 3.governor 4.Oklahoma 5.Oklahoma City

Buzzing Around Oklahoma!

Write the answers to the questions below. To get to the beehive, follow a path through the maze in the same order as your answers.

1. Near the Oklahoma-Arkansas border, you can see the _________________________ Mounds.
2. Oklahoma was bought by the United States as part of the _________________________ Purchase.
3. The capital of Oklahoma is _________________________ City.
4. Oklahoma is the _________________________ state.
5. The highest point in Oklahoma is _________________________ Mesa.
6. The longest river in Oklahoma is the North _________________________ River.
7. The first capital of Oklahoma was _________________________.
8. During the drought of the 1920s and 1930s, Oklahoma was part of the ______________ ______________.
9. The first people to live in Oklahoma were the American____________________.
10. The _________________________ River runs along Oklahoma's southern border.

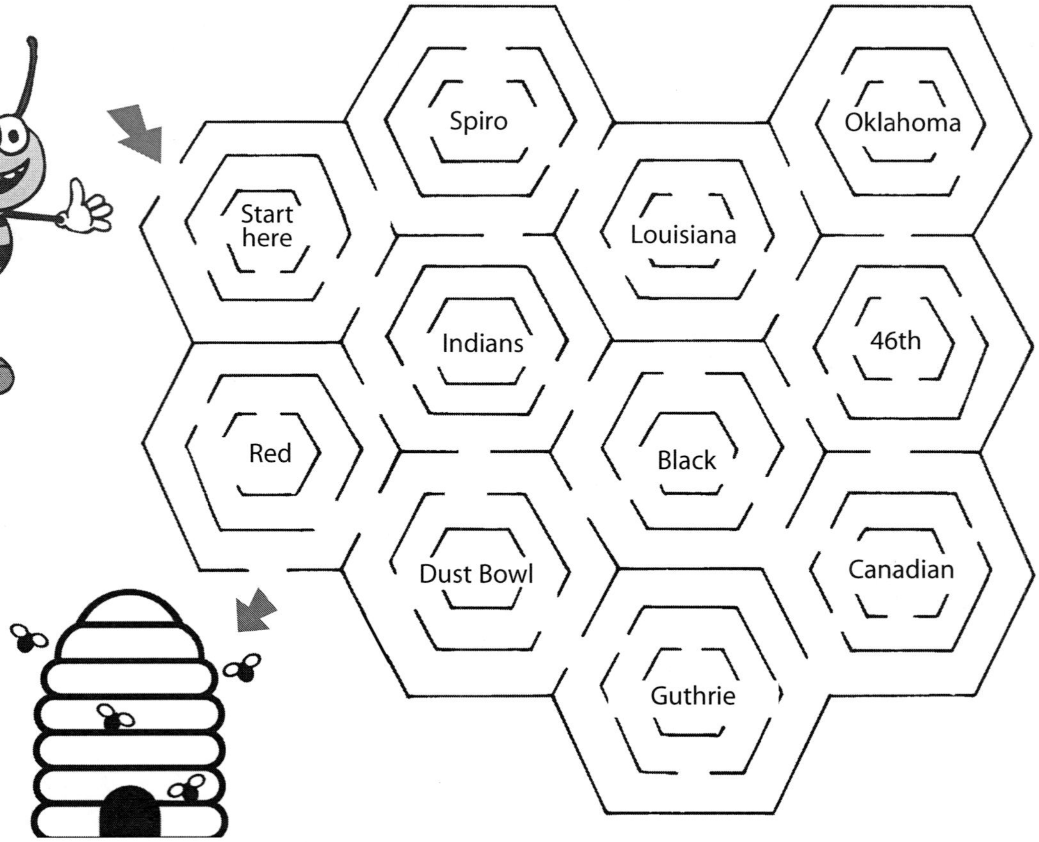

ANSWERS: 1.Spiro 2.Louisiana 3.Oklahoma 4.46th 5.Black 6.Canadian 7.Guthrie 8.Dust Bowl 9.Indians 10.Red

Oklahoma Through the Years!

Many great things have happened in Oklahoma throughout its history. Chronicle the following important Oklahoma events by solving math problems to find out the years in which they happened.

1. Coronado claims the western half of the Mississippi River Valley for Spain
   2-1= 3+2= 2x2= 9-8=
2. La Salle claims the area including Oklahoma for France
   7-6= 4+2= 7+1= 7-5=
3. The United States buys land including Oklahoma from France
   9-8= 2x4= 9-9= 2+1=
4. Fort Gibson and Towson are founded
   3÷3= 6+2= 4-2= 3+1=
5. Congress passes the Indian Removal Act
   6-5= 3+5= 3-0= 4-4=
6. The first Land Run takes place
   1+0= 2+6= 8+0= 3x3=
7. The first commercial oil well is drilled in Bartlesville
   3-2= 7+1= 5+4= 4+3=
8. Oklahoma becomes part of the Dust Bowl
   5-4= 3+6= 2+1= 6-6=
9. Oklahoma is the first state to limit legislators' terms
   6-5= 5+4= 8+1= 5-5=
10. The Murrah Federal Building in Oklahoma City is bombed
    7÷7= 9+0= 6+3= 3+2=

ANSWERS: 1.1541 2.1682 3.1803 4.1824 5.1830 6.1889 7.1897 8.1930 9.1990 10.1995

Festive Oklahoma!

Every year, Oklahomans have a wide variety of festivals, fairs, and events to choose from. **See if you can match these events with the city or town in which they are held.**

1. Chocolate Festival — A. Bartlesville
2. World Championship Hog Calling Contest — B. Oklahoma City
3. Eighty-Niner Day Celebration — C. Enid
4. Strawberry Festival — D. Guthrie
5. OK Mozart Festival — E. Norman
6. Red Earth Festival — F. Weatherford
7. Annual Rodeo and Old Cowhand Reunion — G. Freedom
8. Cherokee Strip Celebration — H. Stillwell

ANSWERS: 1.E 2.F 3.D 4.H 5.A 6.B 7.G 8.C

Rhymin' Riddles!

1. I am the Sooner State, my name starts with an "O";
   In the 1800s, I was the end of the Trail of Tears and woe.

   What am I? ______________________

2. We stretch across the land, so high and so wide;
   In northeast Oklahoma a beautiful sight we provide.

   What are we? ____________ ______________

3. We fought for the Union, at the Battle of Honey Springs;
   We also fought bandits, Indians, all manner of things.

   Who are we? ____________ ______________

4. We lived in Oklahoma before the explorers did roam;
   On the lands near rivers and plains were our tribes' home.

   Who are we? ______________________

ANSWERS: 1.Oklahoma 2.Ozark Mountains 3.Buffalo Soldiers 4.Indians

Oklahoma's Venomous Snakes!

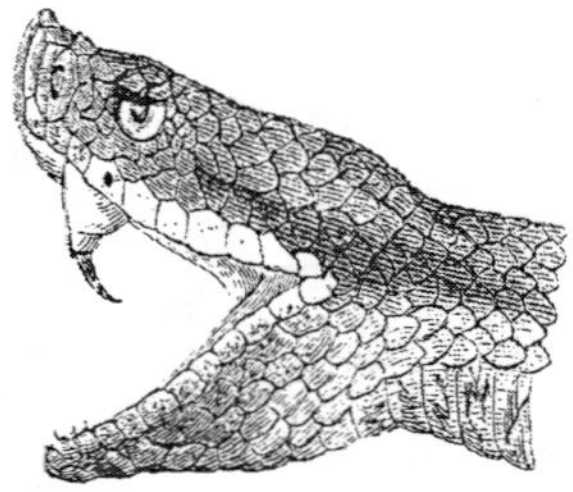

Three types of venomous (poisonous) snakes live in Oklahoma.

Using the alphabet code, see if you can find out their names.

A	B	C	D	E	F	G	H	I	J	K	L	M	N	O	P	Q	R	S	T
1	2	3	4	5	6	7	8	9	10	11	12	13	14	15	16	17	18	19	20

U	V	W	X	Y	Z
21	22	23	24	25	26

1. ___ ___ ___ ___ ___ ___ ___ ___ ___ ___ ___
18 1 20 20 12 5 19 14 1 11 5

2. ___ ___ ___ ___ ___ ___ ___ ___ ___ ___
3 15 16 16 5 18 8 5 1 4

3. ___ ___ ___ ___ ___ ___ ___ ___ ___ ___ ___
3 15 20 20 15 14 13 15 21 20 8

ANSWERS: 1.rattlesnake 2.copperhead 3.cottonmouth

Historical Oklahoma Women!

Oklahoma has been the home of many brave and influential women.

See if you can match these women with their accomplishments. Write the letter of each woman's accomplishment next to her name.

1. Angie Debo
2. Wilma Mankiller
3. Alice Mary Robertson
4. Shannon Miller
5. Mattie Beal
6. Shannon Lucid

A. Olympic gymnast and gold medalist

B. U.S. Representative from 1921 to 1923

C. known as the "First Lady of Oklahoma History"

D. first female Principal Chief of the Cherokee Nation

E. astronaut

F. was second-place winner in the Oklahoma Land Lottery of 1901

ANSWERS: 1.C 2.D 3.B 4.A 5.F 6.E

Oklahoma Word Wheel!

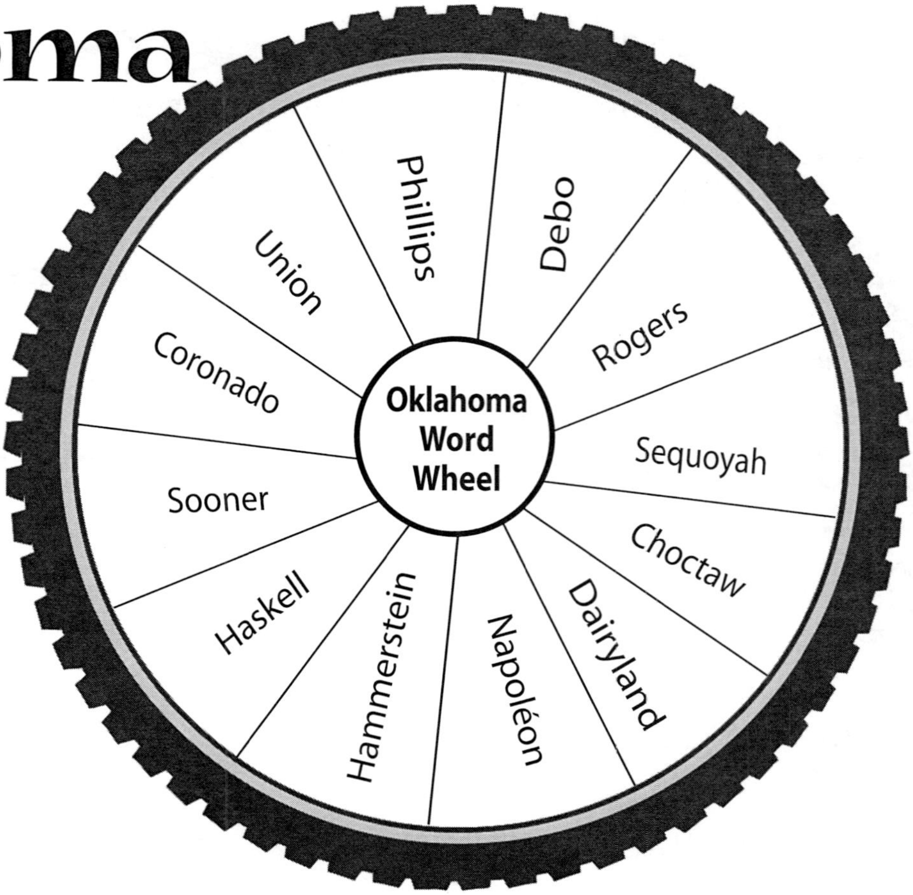

Use the Word Wheel of Oklahoma names to complete the sentences below.

1. In the 1540s, Francisco Vásquez de ____________________ led an expedition into the Colorado area looking for gold.
2. Oklahoma and the rest of the Louisiana Purchase was sold to the United States by ____________________ Bonaparte.
3. The man who created an alphabet for the Cherokee language was ____________________.
4. The first governor of the state of Oklahoma was Charles N. ____________________.
5. The newspaper columnist Will ____________________ grew up near what is now Oologah, Oklahoma.
6. Oklahoma's state song was written by Richard Rodgers and Oscar ____________________.
7. Angie ____________________ is known as the First Lady of Oklahoma History.
8. The Five Civilized Tribes of Oklahoma were the Cherokee, ____________________, Creek, Seminole, and Chickasaw.
9. Oklahoma is known as the ____________________ State.
10. The first commercial oil well in Oklahoma was drilled by Frank ____________________ in 1897.

ANSWERS: 1.Coronado 2.Napoléon 3.Sequoyah 4.Haskell 5.Rogers 6.Hammerstein 7.Debo 8.Choctaw 9.Sooner 10.Phillips

Oklahoma Tour Guide!

Pretend that you are a professional tour guide. Your job is to find interesting and educational things for visitors to see and do in the state. For the following list of cities, find at least one attraction, activity, or event that a tourist can visit or do. You may need to use an encyclopedia, almanac, or other source to find the information.

Pawhuska

____

Shawnee

____

Tahlequah

____

Tishomingo

____

Write the name of your Oklahoma town here.

____

Now write down at least one thing a tourist can see or do in your town. If your town is already on the list, think of a different thing for tourists to do.

____

____

____

____

Mixed-Up States!

Color, cut out, and paste each of Oklahoma's six neighbors onto the map.

Be sure and match the state shapes!

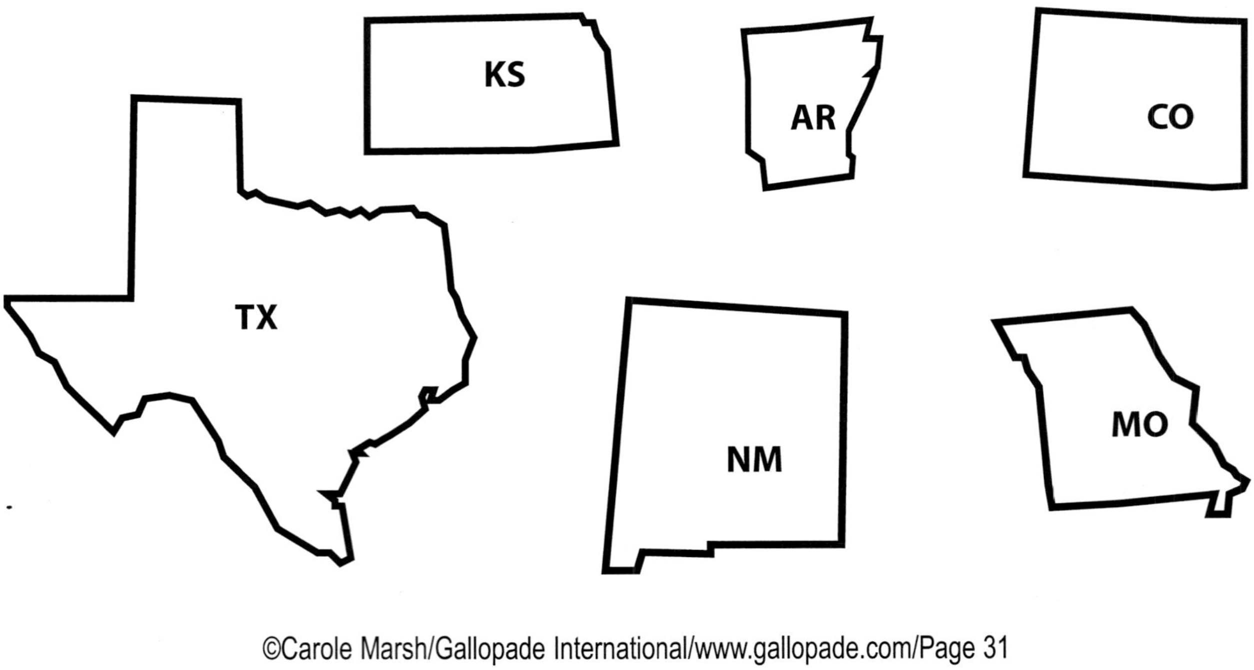

Oklahoma-Chat!

Some people in Oklahoma use words and expressions that are part of Southern Highland or Southern Midland speech. These colloquial or conversational words come from the southern part of the Appalachian Mountains and were brought by settlers to Oklahoma.

Here are just a few. See if you can match the Southern Midland words and phrases on the left with their meanings on the right.

1. critter	____	A. wrestle
2. a-goin	____	B. creature
3. wrassle	____	C. children
4. young-uns	____	D. getting ready to do something
5. skift	____	E. confused
6. fixin' to	____	F. going
7. sparkin'	____	G. a dusting of snow
8. bumfuzzled	____	H. courting/flirting

ANSWERS: 1.B 2.F 3.A 4.C 5.G 6.D 7.H 8.E

Create Your Own Quarter!

Look at the change in your pocket. You might notice that one of the coins has changed. The United States is minting new quarters, one for each of the fifty states. Each quarter has a design on it that says something special about one particular state. That means that Oklahoma will have its very own state quarter!

What do you think should go on the Oklahoma quarter? Draw a picture of how you would like the Oklahoma quarter to look. Make sure you include things that are special about Oklahoma.

Oklahoma's Governor!

The governor is the leader of the state.

Do some research to complete this biography of the governor.

Governor's name:

____

Paste a picture of the governor here: ➤

The governor was born in this state:

____

The governor was born on this date:

____

Members of the governor's family:

____

____

Interesting facts about the governor:

____

____

____

____

____

____

____

____

States All Around Code-Buster!

Decipher the code and write in the names of the states that border Oklahoma.

A	B	C	D	E	F	G	H	I	J	K	L	M	N	O	P	Q	R
✹	❀	✣	♣	➳	❤	❢	✲	✂	✆	☛	✈	✉	✿	✩	✦	✡	✎

S	T	U	V	W	X	Y	Z
❦	☎	✒	✚	✖	✍	✠	✓

1. ___ ___ ___ ___ ___ ___
☛ ✹ ✿ ❦ ✹ ❦

2. ___ ___ ___ ___ ___ ___ ___ ___
✹ ✎ ☛ ✹ ✿ ❦ ✹ ❦

3. ___ ___ ___ ___ ___
☎ ➳ ✍ ✹ ❦

4. ___ ___ ___ ___ ___ ___ ___ ___
✣ ✩ ✈ ✩ ✎ ✹ ♣ ✩

5. ___ ___ ___   ___ ___ ___ ___ ___ ___
✿ ➳ ✖   ✉ ➳ ✍ ✂ ✣ ✩

6. ___ ___ ___ ___ ___ ___ ___ ___
✉ ✂ ❦ ❦ ✩ ✒ ✎ ✂

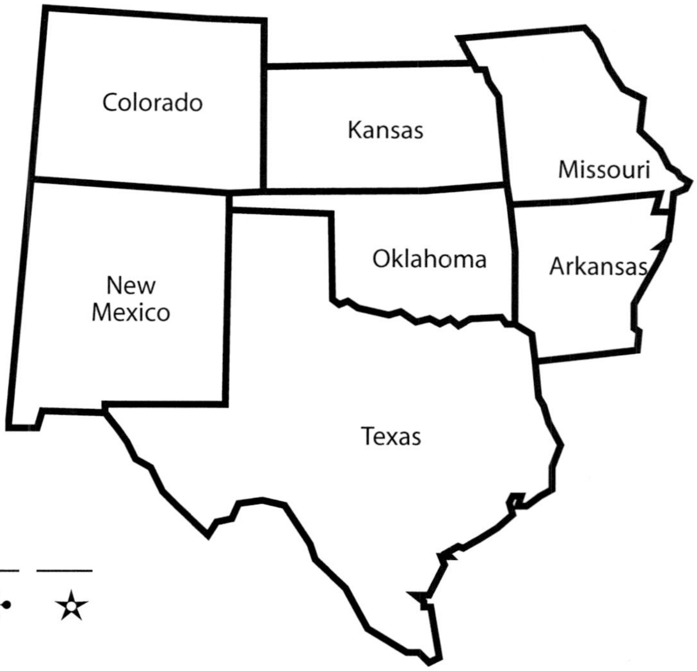

ANSWERS: 1.Kansas 2.Arkansas 3.Texas 4.Colorado 5.New Mexico 6.Missouri

One-of-a-Kind Oklahoma Place Names!

Can you figure out the compound words that make up the names of these Oklahoma cities?

BETHANY	BLACKWELL	CANTON
________ ________	________ ________	________ ________
DRUMRIGHT	FAIRFAX	FAIRVIEW
________ ________	________ ________	________ ________
GOODLAND	GRANDFIELD	MANGUM
________ ________	________ ________	________ ________
STILLWATER	STONEWALL	NEWCASTLE
________ ________	________ ________	________ ________
	HINTON	GOODWELL
	________ ________	________ ________

Looking For a Home!

Draw a line from the things on the left to their homes on the right!

1. Oklahoma's governor
2. cowboy wannabe
3. enterprising businessperson
4. howitzer gunner
5. gorillas and dolphins
6. Oklahoma Sooners
7. bison
8. hikers and mountain bikers
9. African-American bronco riders
10. archaeology and paleontology enthusiasts

A. Fort Sill
B. Tallgrass Prairie Preserve
C. Ozark Mountains
D. Sam Noble Oklahoma Museum of Natural History
E. Enterprise Square, USA
F. National Cowboy Hall of Fame
G. Oklahoma City
H. Memorial Stadium
I. Black Invitational Rodeo
J. Oklahoma City Zoo

ANSWERS: 1.G 2.F 3.E 4.A 5.J 6.H 7.B 8.C 9.I 10.D

Weather, or not!

Oklahoma has a temperate, or mild, climate. It's usually cool in the north, warm in the south, and dry in the west. The highest temperature ever recorded was 120°F (49°C) in 1936, but the average July temperature is usually around 82°F (28°C). The growing season is usually quite long in Oklahoma.

The coldest Oklahoma temperature was recorded in 1904, when it dropped to -27°F (-33°C)! Usually, Winter temperatures in January are around 37°F (3°C).

On the thermometer gauges below, color the mercury red (°F) to show the hottest temperature ever recorded in Oklahoma. Color the mercury blue (°F) to show the coldest temperature ever recorded in Oklahoma.

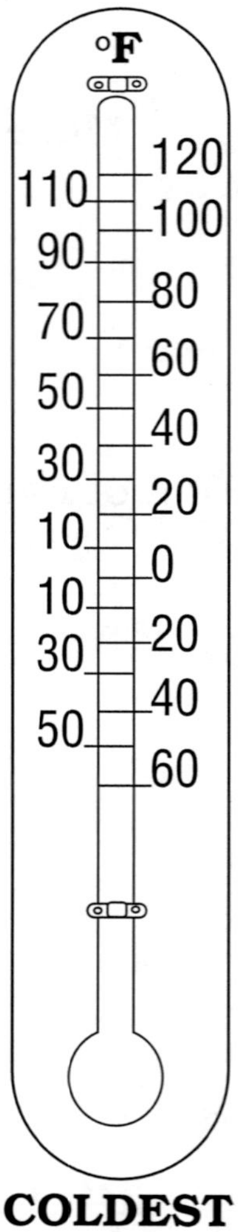

COLDEST

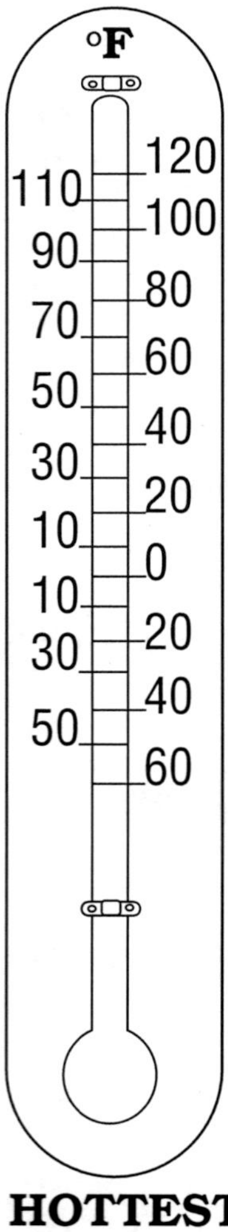

HOTTEST

The Scenic Route!

Imagine that you are planning a field trip for your class and you're taking your classmates on a trip to some famous Oklahoma places.

Circle these sites and cities on the map below, then number them in the order you would visit if you were traveling north to south through the state:

_____Oklahoma City

_____Lake Texoma

_____Osage Reservation

_____Tulsa

_____Eufaula Lake

_____Muskogee

_____Wichita Mountains

_____Broken Arrow

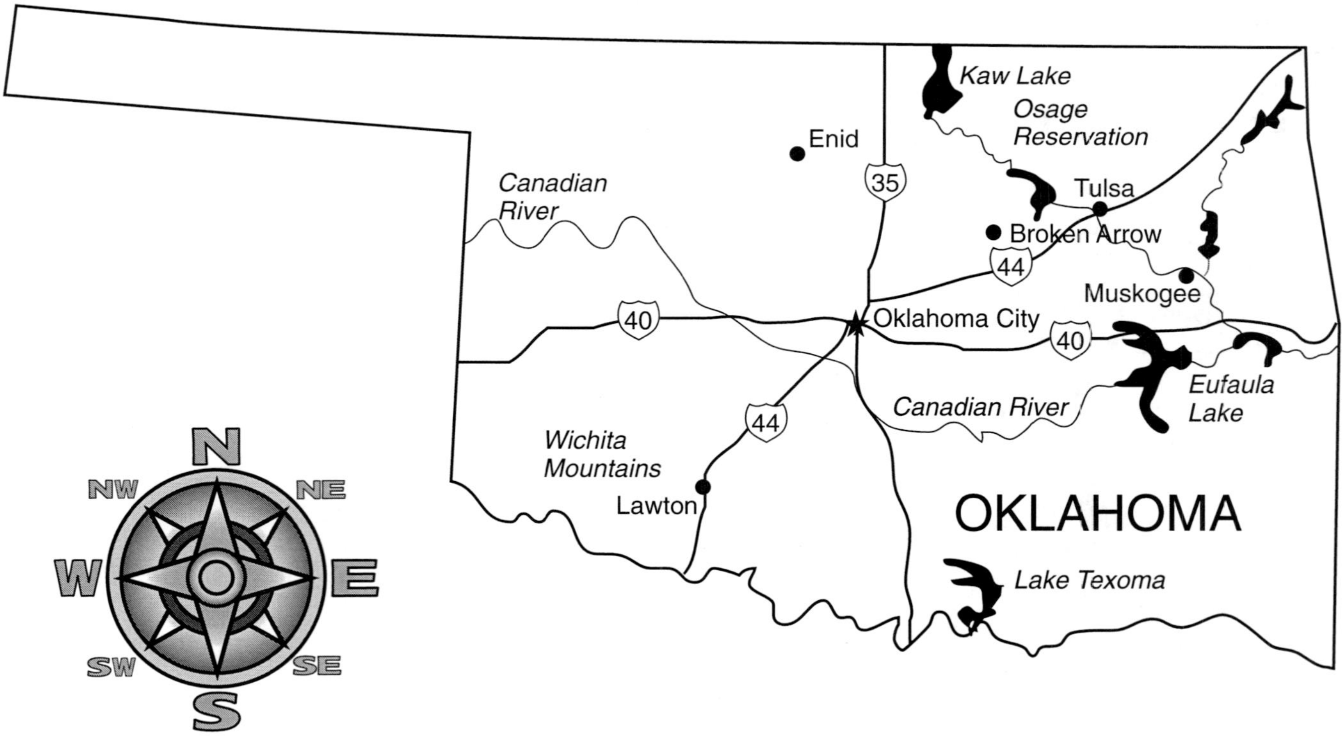

ANSWERS: 1.Osage Reservation 2.Tulsa 3.Broken Arrow 4.Muskogee 5.Oklahoma City 6.Eufaula Lake 7.Wichita Mountains 8.Lake Texoma

Depression + Dust = New Deal!

After the collapse of the stock market on Wall Street in 1929, the state of Oklahoma, along with the rest of the nation, went into the Great Depression. It was the worst economic crisis America had ever known. Banks closed and businesses failed. Oklahoma was one of the hardest-hit states, because it was already in economic trouble before the Great Depression even began. During the 1930s, a severe drought struck the Midwest. Without rain, the land's topsoil blew away in windstorms. These storms were called the Dust Bowl. It left no hope for Oklahoma farmers trying to raise crops.

Our President Helps

While the nation was in the midst of the Depression, Franklin Delano Roosevelt became president. The federal government hired unemployed people to build parks, bridges, and roads. With this help, and other government assistance, the country began to slowly, and painfully, pull out of the Great Depression. Within the first 100 days of his office, Roosevelt enacted a number of policies to help minimize the suffering of the nation's many unemployed workers. These programs were known as the NEW DEAL. The jobs helped families support themselves and improved the country's infrastructure.

Put an X next to the jobs that were part of Roosevelt's New Deal.

1. computer programmer ________
2. bridge builder ________
3. fashion model ________
4. park builder ________
5. interior designer ________
6. hospital builder ________
7. school builder ________
8. website designer ________

ANSWERS: 2 4 6 7

The First Americans

When European explorers first arrived in America, they found many Native American tribes living here.

Shawnee Indians lived in the Eastern Woodlands region of the United States. The types of homes they lived in were wigwams. **Color the Eastern Woodlands green.**

Plains Indians lived in Oklahoma in the Great Plains region of North America. Some Plains Indians lived in teepees. **Color the Great Plains yellow.**

Pueblo Indians lived in the Southwest region of North America. They lived in multi-story terraced buildings, called pueblos. **Color the Southwest red.**

The Five Civilized Tribes lived in the Southeast region of the United States. They lived in rectangular thatched houses called wattle and daub. **Color the Southeast blue.**

Color these houses Indians lived in. Then draw a line from the type of house to the correct region.

Oklahoma Immigration

People have come to Oklahoma from many other states and countries. As time has gone by, Oklahoma's population has grown more diverse. This means that people of different races and from different cultures and ethnic backgrounds have moved to Oklahoma.

At the end of the Civil War, many African-Americans moved from the South to the Indian Territory (Oklahoma) to start their own businesses and homesteads. Many of the Native Americans who were displaced by the Indian Removal Act also moved to Oklahoma. Most recently, people have immigrated from Hispanic, Asian, and Pacific countries. Only a certain number of immigrants are allowed to move to America each year. Many of these immigrants eventually become U.S. citizens.

Read the statement and decide if it's a fact or an opinion. Write your answer on the line.

1. Many of Oklahoma's early residents came from the South. ____________________
2. Lots of immigrants speak a language other than English. ____________________
3. The clothing immigrants wear is very interesting. ____________________
4. Immigrants from China have a neat accent when they speak. ____________________
5. Many immigrants will become United States citizens. ____________________
6. Many recent immigrants come from the Pacific Islands and Asia. ____________________

ANSWERS: 1.Fact 2.Fact 3.Opinion 4.Opinion 5.Fact 6.Fact

This Old House!

Take yourself back 100 years. Can you imagine what life would be like in the Victorian Era? What did turn-of-the-century Oklahomans own? How did they live? See if you can pick out which of the following items people at the turn of the century had and which ones they did not.

Circle the things you might find or use around your 1900 home.

ANSWERS: 1, 2, 3, 4, 6, 7, 9, 10, 11, 13, 15, 16, 17, 18, 19, 20, 22

Home, Sweet Home!

Match these famous Oklahoma authors with their native or adopted hometowns. Some may be used more than once.

A = McAlester B = Oklahoma City C = Oklahoma Territory
D = Lawton E = Tulsa

______ 1. **Ralph Ellison:** African-American novelist and essayist, a library is named in his honor in his hometown

______ 2. **Tony Hillerman:** has written many books and stories about the Navajo Indians

______ 3. **N. Scott Momaday:** Pulitzer Prize-winning author of *House Made of Dawn*

______ 4. **John Hope Franklin:** African-American author

______ 5. **Angie Debo:** the First Lady of Oklahoma History

______ 6. **John Berryman:** Pulitzer Prize-winning poet

ANSWERS: 1.B 2.D 3.D 4.E 5.C 6.A

Oklahoma Spelling Bee!

Good spelling is a good habit. Study the words on the left side of the page. Then fold the page in half and "take a spelling test" on the right side. Have a buddy read the words aloud to you. When done, unfold the page and check your spelling. Keep your score. GOOD LUCK.

agriculture	____________________
archaeology	____________________
bullfrog	____________________
Chisholm	____________________
Coronado	____________________
enterprise	____________________
executive	____________________
flycatcher	____________________
judicial	____________________
legislative	____________________
mistletoe	____________________
Okmulgee	____________________
segregation	____________________
Shawnee	____________________
territory	____________________
tornado	____________________
university	____________________

Sooner Women's Suffrage!

Before the 19th Amendment to the United States Constitution, women were unable to vote in the United States. However, in 1918, the state of Oklahoma did grant women the right to vote. In 1920, enough states ratified the 19th Amendment and it became the law of the land. Women gained total suffrage nationally. Women today continue to be a major force in the election process.

Match the words in the left box with their definitions in the right box.

1. Amendment ______
2. Ratify ______
3. Constitution ______
4. State Senate ______
5. Law of the Land ______
6. Election ______
7. Suffrage ______
8. Women ______

A. The right to vote

B. A law that is an acceptable practice throughout the nation

C. People who could not vote in Oklahoma until 1918

D. An addition to the U.S. Constitution

E. The selection, by vote, of a candidate for office

F. To give approval

G. The fundamental law of the United States that was framed in 1787 and put into effect in 1789

H. One half of Oklahoma's state legislature

ANSWERS: 1.D 2.F 3.G 4.H 5.B 6.E 7.A 8.C

Naturally Oklahoma!

Fill in the bubblegram with some of our state's crops and natural resources. Use the first and last letter clues to help you.

WORD BANK

LIVESTOCK
WHEAT
FRUIT
LIMESTONE
COTTON
PECANS
COAL

1. ◯ ◯ __ L
2. C ◯ __ __ __ ◯
3. L __ ◯ __ __ ◯ __ __ K
4. P __ __ ◯ __ ◯
5. L ◯ __ __ __ __ __ ◯ __
6. __ ◯ __ __ T
7. W __ ◯ __ __

Now unscramble the "bubble" letters to find out the mystery word!
HINT: What is one way we can help to save our environment?

__ __ __ __ __ __ __ __ __ __ __ __

MYSTERY WORD: CONSERVATION
ANSWERS: 1.COAL 2.COTTON 3.LIVESTOCK 4.PECANS 5.LIMESTONE 6.FRUIT 7.WHEAT

Digging for Profit!

Oklahoma's primary industry is the mining of natural resources. The state has large coal, petroleum, and natural gas reserves. Ever since oil was discovered there in the late 19th century, Oklahoma has been a major oil producer in the United States. In fact, the first commercial oil well was drilled in Bartlesville way back in 1891! Oil is found under much of Oklahoma, and bituminous coal is found throughout the eastern part of the state. Oklahoma also mines salt, gypsum, limestone, red granite, sand, gravel, and clays. Helium, which is a by-product of natural gas, is also produced in Oklahoma!

Put the names of these minerals found in Oklahoma in alphabetical order, by numbering them 1 to 10.

_____ gravel

_____ limestone

_____ salt

_____ coal

_____ sand

_____ clay

_____ gypsum

_____ granite

_____ natural gas

_____ petroleum

ANSWERS: 1.clay 2.coal 3.granite 4.gravel 5.gypsum 6.limestone 7.natural gas 8.petroleum 9.salt 10.sand

What a Great Idea!

These are just some of the amazing Oklahoma inventions and inventors.

WORD BANK

parking	cart
yield	radio
alphabet	

1. The first shopping ___ ___ ___ ___ was developed by an Oklahoman named Sylvan Goldman.

2. Sequoyah developed an ___ ___ ___ ___ ___ ___ ___ ___ for the Cherokee language.

3. Oklahoma City had the first ___ ___ ___ ___ ___ ___ ___ meter in 1935.

4. Karl Jansky was the first to detect ___ ___ ___ ___ ___ waves from space.

5. Clinton Riggs designed the ___ ___ ___ ___ ___ sign, and first tested it in Tulsa.

ANSWERS: 1.cart 2.alphabet 3.parking 4.radio 5.yield

Famous Oklahoman Scavenger Hunt!

Here is a list of some of the famous people associated with our state. Go on a scavenger hunt to see if you can "capture" a fact about each one. Use an encyclopedia, almanac, or other resource you might need. Happy hunting!

FAMOUS PERSON	FAMOUS FACT
Carl Bert Albert	
William B. Bizzell	
Ralph Waldo Ellison	
Woody Guthrie	
Patrick Jay Hurley	
Karl Jansky	
Robert Kerr	
Wilma Mankiller	
Mickey Mantle	
N. Scott Momaday	
Frank Phillips	
Oral Roberts	
Alice Mary Robertson	
Will Rogers	
Sequoyah	
Maria Tallchief	
James Francis Thorpe	

The Great Dust Storm!

(from *Dust Bowl Ballads*, by Woody Guthrie)

Use the words from the Word Bank to fill in the blanks in the song lyrics below. Some words may be used more than once.

WORD BANK

black **doom**

storm **dust**

Oklahoma

On the fourteenth day of April, in nineteen thirty five,

There struck the worst of _ _ _ _ _ _ _ _ _s that ever filled the sky.

You could see the _ _ _ _ _ _ _ _ _ comin', the cloud was death-like _ _ _ _ _,

And through our mighty nation it left a dreadful track.

From _ _ _ _ _ _ _ _ City to the Arizona Line,

The corner of Nebrasky to the lazy Rio Grande,

It fell across our city like a curtain of _ _ _ _ _ rolled down.

We thought it was our judgment, we thought it was our _ _ _ _.

The radio reported. We listened with alarm

To the wild and windy actions of this great mysterious _ _ _ _ _.

From Albuquerq' and Clovis and all New Mexico,

They said it was the _ _ _ _ _est they had ever saw.

Map of North America

This is a map of North America. Oklahoma is one of the 50 states.

Color the state of Oklahoma red.

Color the rest of the United States yellow. Alaska and Hawaii are part of the United States and should also be colored yellow.

Color Canada green. Color Mexico blue.

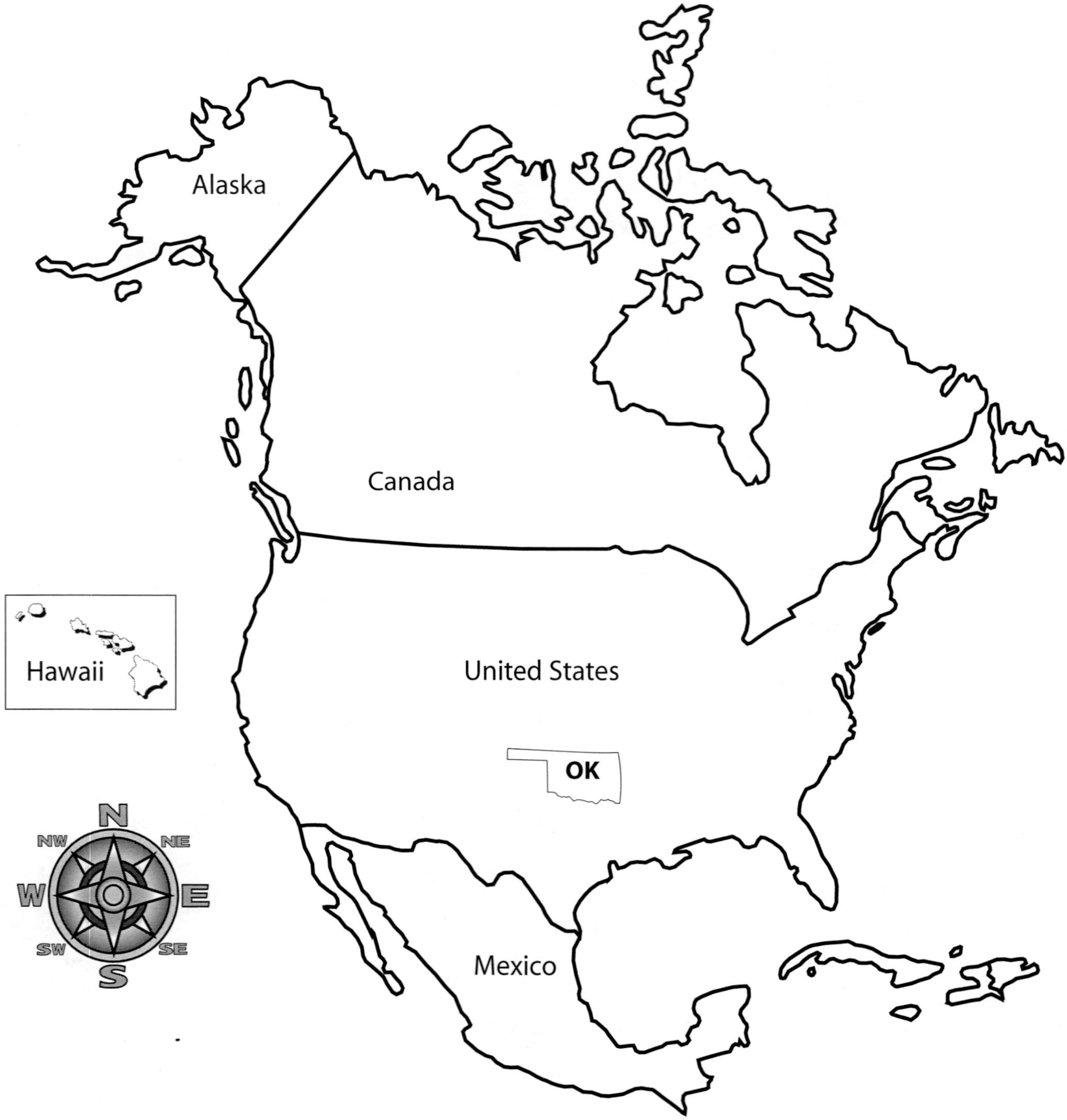

Oklahornado!

Tornadoes are a regular part of Oklahoma's climate. Masses of warm, moist air collide with masses of cold, dry air in the skies over the state. These collisions can produce violent thunderstorms, and sometimes tornadoes. On May 15, 1990, six tornadoes and eight funnels were sighted in Oklahoma. The worst ripped through Stillwater, with winds of more than 100 miles (161 kilometers) per hour. It destroyed or damaged more than 600 houses and apartments in the city. Oklahoma has the fourth most tornadoes in the United States every year – between 1950 and 1987 alone, more than 2,000 tornadoes hit Oklahoma!

For each of these tornado survival "tips," circle whether it would be a GOOD or a BAD idea during a tornado.

1. GOOD BAD Going into a walk-in closet
2. GOOD BAD Standing outside and watching the storm
3. GOOD BAD Going down into the basement
4. GOOD BAD Ignoring tornado warnings on the radio
5. GOOD BAD Moving away from windows
6. GOOD BAD Going up to the top floor of your house

ANSWERS: 1.good 2.bad 3.good 4.bad 5.good 6.bad

The Slopes of the Sooner State!

Oklahoma's topography generally slopes from the highest point, Black Mesa (4,973 feet or 1,516 meters) in the northwest to the lowest point (287 feet or 87 meters) in the far southeastern corner of the state. The Ouachita Mountains in the southeast have peaks that reach as high as 2,600 feet (800 meters). Areas of the Ozark Plateau have elevations as high as 1,200 feet (365 meters). Oklahoma is also the home of the world's tallest hill! In order for a mountain to be called a mountain, it has to be 2,000 feet (600 meters) high. Cavanal Hill in Oklahoma is only 1,999 feet (599.7 meters) high!

Using the information in the paragraph above, graph the elevations (heights), in feet, of the different things listed. The first one has been done for you.

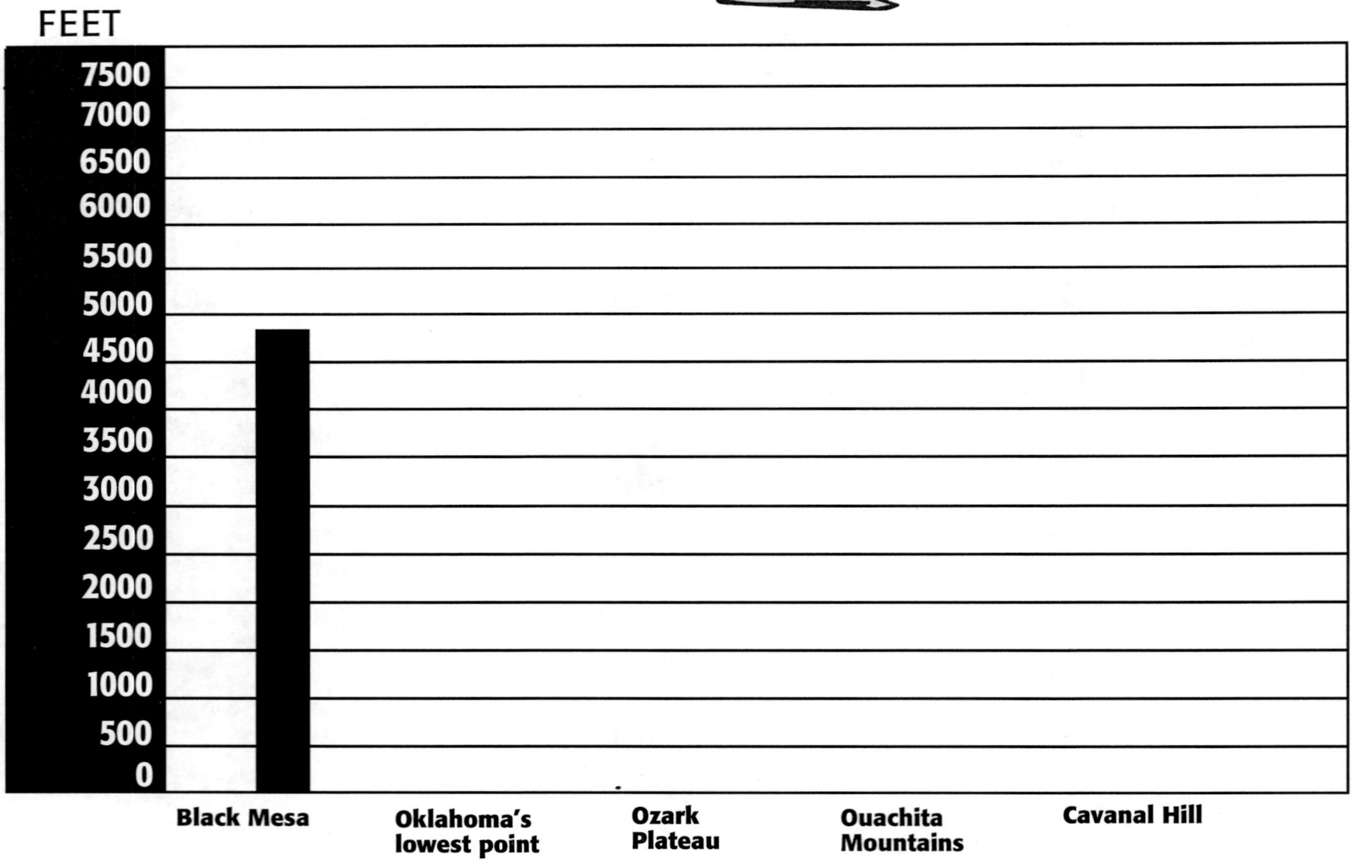

Oklahoma State Greats!

How many of these state greats from the great state of Oklahoma do you know?

Use an encyclopedia, almanac, or other resource to match the following facts with the state great they describe.

Hint: There are two facts for each state great!

_____ 1. president of Oklahoma's constitutional convention

_____ 2. voted the greatest athlete of the half-century in 1950

_____ 3. wrote thirteen books

_____ 4. governor of Oklahoma from 1931 to 1935

_____ 5. one of America's original seven astronauts

_____ 6. prima ballerina of the New York City Ballet from 1947 to 1960

_____ 7. arrived in Oklahoma Territory by covered wagon

_____ 8. won two gold medals in the 1912 Olympics

_____ 9. first astronaut to make two space flights that orbited the earth

_____10. founder of the Chicago City Ballet

STATE GREAT

A. Angie Debo

B. William Henry Murray

C. Maria Tallchief

D. Leroy Gordon Cooper, Jr.

E. James Thorpe

ANSWERS: 1.B 2.E 3.A 4.B 5.D 6.C 7.A 8.E 9.D 10.C

Oklahoma Writers!

Fill in the missing first or last name of these famous Oklahoma writers.

1. First name: Lynn
   Last name: ______________________________
2. First name: ______________________________
   Last name: Axelson
3. First name: Angie
   Last name: ______________________________
4. First name: ______________________________
   Last name: Blanding
5. First name: N. Scott
   Last name: ______________________________
6. First name: ______________________________
   Last name: Franklin
7. First name: Tony
   Last name: ______________________________
8. First name: ______________________________
   Last name: Berryman

ANSWERS: 1.Riggs 2.Mary 3.Debo 4.Don 5.Momaday 6.John Hope 7.Hillerman 8.John

A Barite Rose by Any Other Name. . .

Oklahoma has chosen a beautiful rock as its state rock. It's called the Barite Rose Rock because this stone actually looks a lot like a full-grown rose. In fact, the crystals that are found in the sands of Oklahoma are even called "desert roses."

Barite is a fairly soft, but heavy mineral. It's used to make paint, to help with well drilling, in making glass, and in ceramics. An old Cherokee legend says that the rocks represent the blood of the braves and the tears of the maidens along the Trail of Tears.

What tools would you need if you were a prospector looking for Barite Rose Rocks? Circle the tools you'd need below, and label them. Use the Word Bank to help you.

WORD BANK		
pick	shovel	gloves
pan	boots	mule

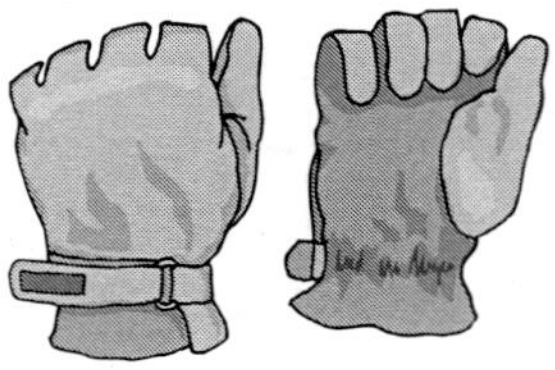

A River Runs Through It!

The state of Oklahoma is blessed with many rivers. See if you can wade right in and figure out which river name completes the sentences below!

WORD BANK

Arkansas	**Beaver**	**Wolf**
Salt Fork	**Canadian**	**Red**

1. I wonder if the _ _ _ _ _ _ _ _ River actually flows from the country it's named after?

2. The _ _ _ River, not the Yellow River, forms the southern border of Oklahoma.

3. I wonder if the _ _ _ _ _ _ River was named after the animals that build dams?

4. When you're on this river, make sure you don't cry _ _ _ _!

5. The _ _ _ _ _ _ _ _ River does actually flow through the state with the same name.

6. Maybe the _ _ _ _ _ _ _ _ River is named after two things we see on the dinner table.

ANSWERS: 1.Canadian 2.Red 3.Beaver 4.Wolf 5.Arkansas 6.Salt Fork

Outstanding Oklahoma Trivia!

HOLD ON!
During a tornado in Ponca City, a man and his wife were swept up into the air from the floor of their house, and eventually glided downward safely to the ground!

LIGHTS, CAMERA, ACTION!
Oklahoma was the setting for the movie *Twister.*

WHAT'S IN A NAME?
Oklahoma is one of only two states where the capital city's name contains the state's name. The other is Indianapolis, Indiana.

ONE, TWO, THREE...
Fourteen flags have flown over Oklahoma!

HOE-DOWN!
The Fiddle is Oklahoma's official state musical instrument.

I CLAIM THEE...
Norman, Oklahoma is named after the words "Norman's Camp" that the young surveyor Abner E. Norman burned into a tree trunk in 1870.

WOODY?
The first capital of Oklahoma was Guthrie.

Now write down another fact that you know about Oklahoma.

____

____

____

Oklahomans In Sp-a-a-a-a-a-ace!

Several of NASA's astronauts have been Oklahomans! Leroy Gordon Cooper, Jr. of Shawnee was one of the seven original astronauts in 1959. He also was the first to make two space flights that orbited the earth! William Pogue of Okemah has shared the American record for the longest space flight (84 days)! Thomas Stafford of Weatherford piloted Gemini 6 during the first space rendezvous. He also commanded the 1975 Apollo-Soyuz Test Project, which was the first space meeting between U.S. astronauts and cosmonauts of the former Soviet Union. Shannon Lucid of Bethany has been an astronaut since 1978, and holds the United States record for the most flight hours in orbit by a woman.

Here is an astronaut ready for his first walk on the moon. Label the parts of his clothing and tools. Use the Word Bank to help you.

WORD BANK

helmet
boots
gloves
lunar module
lunar rover

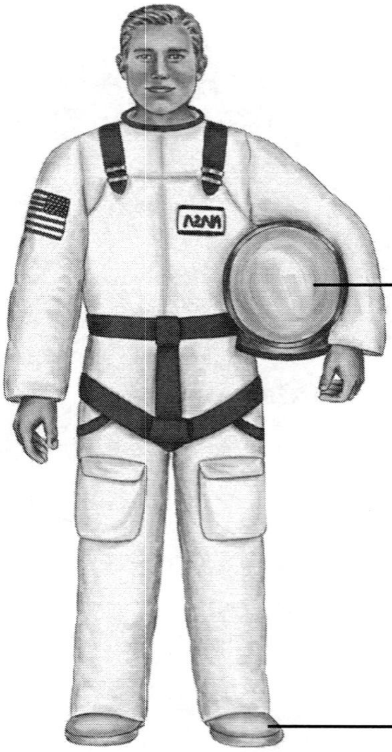

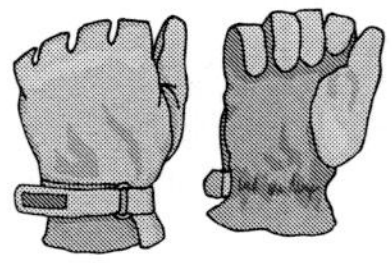

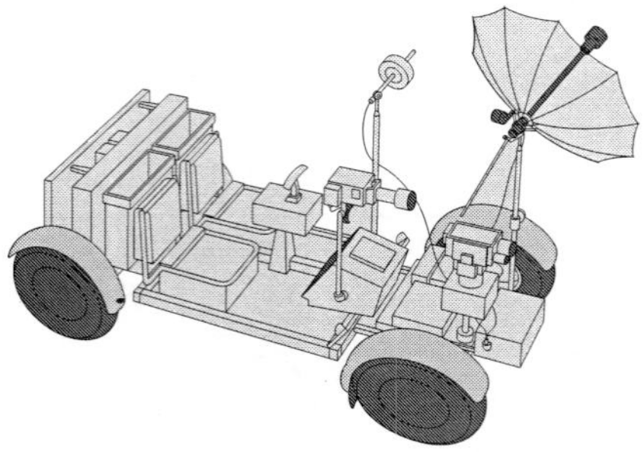

Oklahoma Gazetteer!

A gazetteer is a list of places. **Use the word bank to complete the names of some of these famous places in our state.**

1. _ _ _ _ _ _ City, USA, in Anadarko
2. Fort _ _ _ _, first built as Camp Wichita by the Buffalo Soldiers
3. The _ _ _ _ _ _ _ _ _ Museum of Art in Tulsa
4. The _ _ _ _ _ _ _ _ Science Museum at Oklahoma City
5. The Oklahoma _ _ _ _ _ _ _ _ _ _ _ _ Museum
6. _ _ _ _ _ _ _ _ Stadium, home of the Sooners
7. The Oklahoma _ _ _ _ _ _ _ _ _ _ _ Museum in Guthrie
8. _ _ _ _ _ Tower, the only skyscraper designed by Frank Lloyd Wright that was actually built

WORD BANK

Philbrook	Memorial	Indian	Territorial
Price	Sill	Omniplex	Firefighters

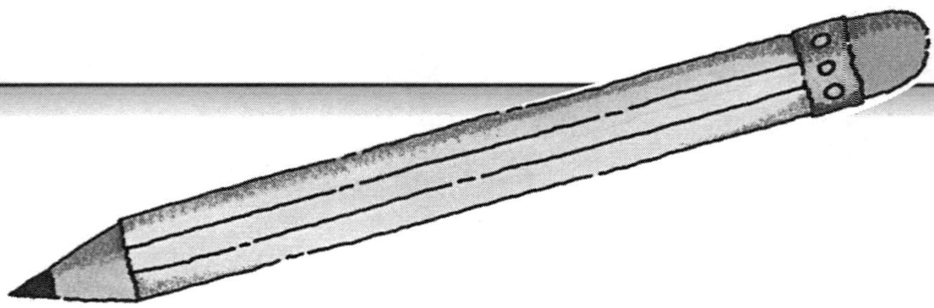

ANSWERS: 1.Indian 2.Sill 3.Philbrook 4.Omniplex 5.Firefighters 6.Memorial 7.Territorial 8.Price

Mixed-up Oklahoma!

Unscramble the words below to get the scoop on all the state symbols of Oklahoma.

1. S L T E I M O T E	____________	STATE FLOWER
2. R O S S S C I – L A I T E D Y F L T C R E H A C	____________ ____________ ____________	STATE BIRD
3. O F U F L B A	____________	STATE ANIMAL
4. T E H I W or N S D A S A S B	____________ ____________	STATE FISH
5. R A I T B E S E O R K C O R	____________ ____________	STATE ROCK
6. B D D E R U	____________	STATE TREE
7. E N E B Y E O H	____________	STATE INSECT
8. N M T I N A U O M E R O B O Z D R I L A	____________ ____________ ____________	STATE REPTILE

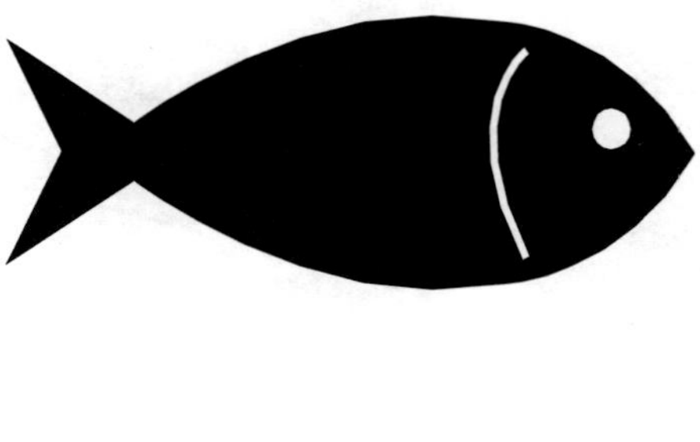

ANSWERS: 1.Mistletoe 2.Scissor-tailed Flycatcher 3.Buffalo 4.White or Sand Bass 5.Barite Rose Rock 6.Redbud 7.Honeybee 8.Mountain Boomer Lizard

Industrious Oklahoma!

Oklahoma's economy is made up of several different industries. Agriculture and oil production are at the heart of Oklahoma's economy, and have been since it was first settled. Mining is also important, and Oklahoma is a major producer of natural gas and coal. Other industries like tourism, manufacturing, construction, and publishing have been recently added to the economy.

Complete these sentences.

Without forestry, I couldn't ______________________________

____

Without rubber, I couldn't ______________________________

____

Without agriculture, I couldn't ______________________________

____

Without food processing, I couldn't ______________________________

____

Without electronics, I couldn't ______________________________

____

Without automobile parts, I couldn't ______________________________

____

Oklahoma Timeline!

A timeline is a list of important events and the year that they happened. You can use a timeline to understand more about history. Read the timeline about Oklahoma history, then see if you can answer the questions at the bottom.

1803..........The United States purchases the Louisiana Territory, which includes Oklahoma
1830..........Indian Removal Act is passed by Congress
1834..........Congress declares most of eastern Oklahoma to be Indian Territory
1861..........Indian Territory joins the Confederacy after the Civil War begins
1889..........The Land Run begins
1897..........Frank Phillips drills Oklahoma's first commercial oil well
1907..........Oklahoma becomes the 46th state
1930..........Many people leave Oklahoma because of the Dust Bowl
1982..........World oil prices drop, affecting Oklahoma's economy
1995..........The Murrah Federal Building in Oklahoma city is bombed

Now put yourself back in the proper year if you were the following people.

1. If you are excited because you were going to Oklahoma to stake out your own parcel of land, the year is ___________.
2. If you are happy because the area you live in just became the 46th state, the year is ___________.
3. If you are horrified to hear that Native Americans are being removed from their lands in the Southeast, the year is ___________.
4. If you are a worker at a petroleum refinery worried because oil prices had dropped, the year is ___________.
5. If you are excited because the United States had just bought an enormous piece of land, the year is ___________.
6. If you are living in Indian Territory and decide to join up with the South in the current war, the year is ___________.
7. If you are a Sooner moving out of Oklahoma because of a terrible drought, the year is ___________.
8. If you are amazed to see a fountain of oil gush from the first oil well, the year is __________.

ANSWER: 1.1889 2.1907 3.1830 4.1982 5.1803 6.1861 7.1930 8.1897

Oklahoma Banks and Bucks, Buckaroo!

Oklahoma banks provide essential financial services. Some of the services that banks provide include:

- They lend money to consumers to purchase goods and services such as houses, cars, and education.
- They lend money to producers who start new businesses.
- They issue credit cards.
- They provide savings accounts and pay interest to savers.
- They provide checking accounts.

Circle whether you would have more, less, or the same amount of money after each event.

1. You deposit your paycheck into your checking account.	MORE	LESS	SAME
2. You put $1,000 in your savings account.	MORE	LESS	SAME
3. You use your credit card to buy new school clothes.	MORE	LESS	SAME
4. You borrow money from the bank to open a toy store.	MORE	LESS	SAME
5. You write a check at the grocery store.	MORE	LESS	SAME
6. You transfer money from checking to savings.	MORE	LESS	SAME

ANSWERS: 1.more 2.more 3.less 4.more 5.less 6.same

I Am A Famous Person From Oklahoma!

From the Word Bank, find my name and fill in the blank.

WORD BANK

Stephen Long
William H. Murray
Wilma Mankiller
Stand Watie
Jesse Chisholm

1. I was a Cherokee tribal leader and also a Confederate general. I was the last Confederate commander to surrender at the end of the Civil War.

   Who am I? ______________________________

2. I was a part-Cherokee trader who carried goods from the East and Europe to trade with the Indians for furs. The trail that I used was later named after me.

   Who am I? ______________________________

3. I led an expedition in 1819 to find the sources of the Arkansas and Red Rivers. I built Fort Smith on the Oklahoma-Arkansas border.

   Who am I? ______________________________

4. I was the governor of Oklahoma during the Dust Bowl years. I worked to solve the unemployment problem and even donated part of my salary to feed the needy.

   Who am I? ______________________________

5. I was born in Rocky Mountain, and was the first woman to serve as Principal Chief of the Cherokee Nation.

   Who am I? ______________________________

ANSWERS: 1.Stand Watie 2.Jesse Chisholm 3.Stephen Long 4.William H. Murray 5.Wilma Mankiller

Oklahoma's Battlefields!

When the Civil War began, the eastern part of Oklahoma was still the Indian Territory. Some of the Indians living there either stayed out of the war entirely, or sided with the Union. However, many of them fought for the Confederacy. Many battles were fought in Indian Territory. The Civil War ended in 1865 when Confederate General Robert E. Lee surrendered to Union General Ulysses S. Grant at the Appomattox Court House in Virginia.

Draw a line from the name of the location in which each battle occurred to the correct place on the map. There are letter clues on the map to help you.

Round Mountain

Honey Springs

Chustenahlah

Cabin Creek

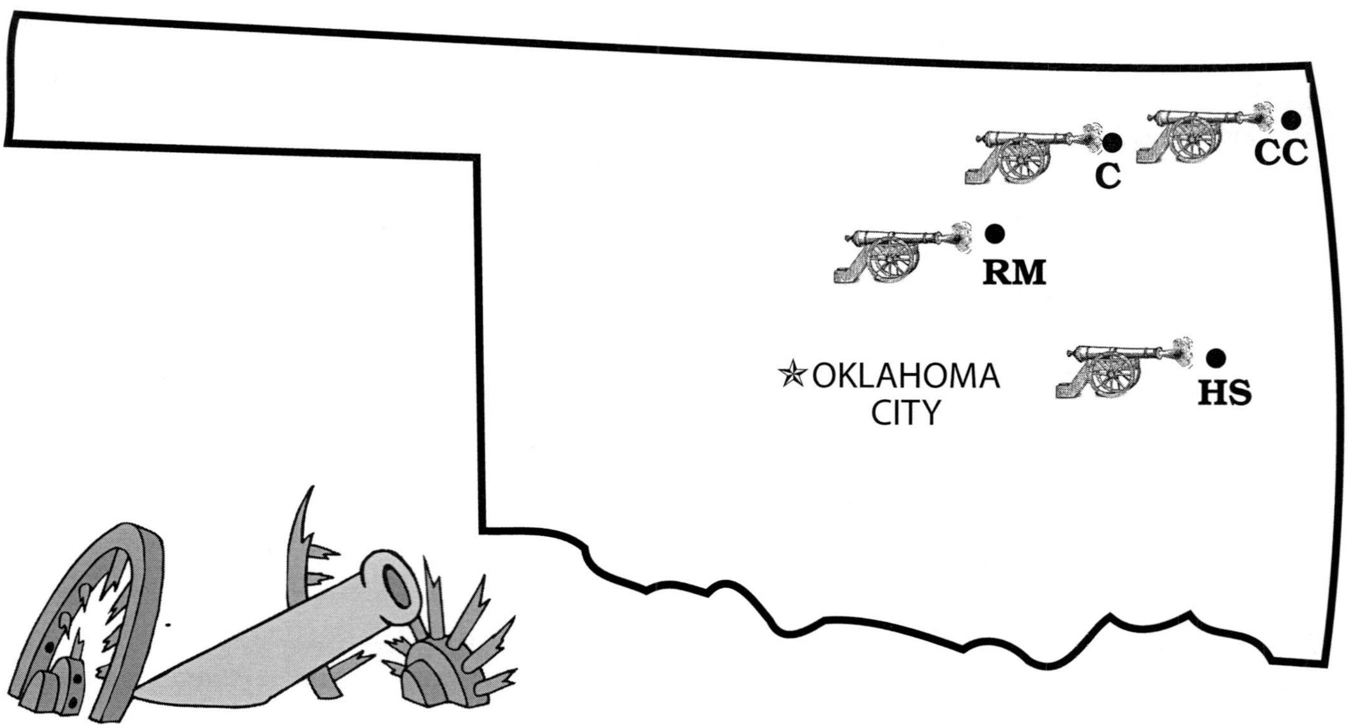

Indians in Oklahoma!

Oklahoma has been the home of several Native American groups. When explorers first arrived, several tribes were already living in the area. In 1830, when the Indian Removal Act was passed, the Five Civilized Tribes were moved into eastern Oklahoma.

Draw a line from the group to its location on the map.

- The Kiowa lived in the Panhandle.
- The Osage lived in the northeastern part of the state.
- The Kiowa-Apache lived in the central part of the state.

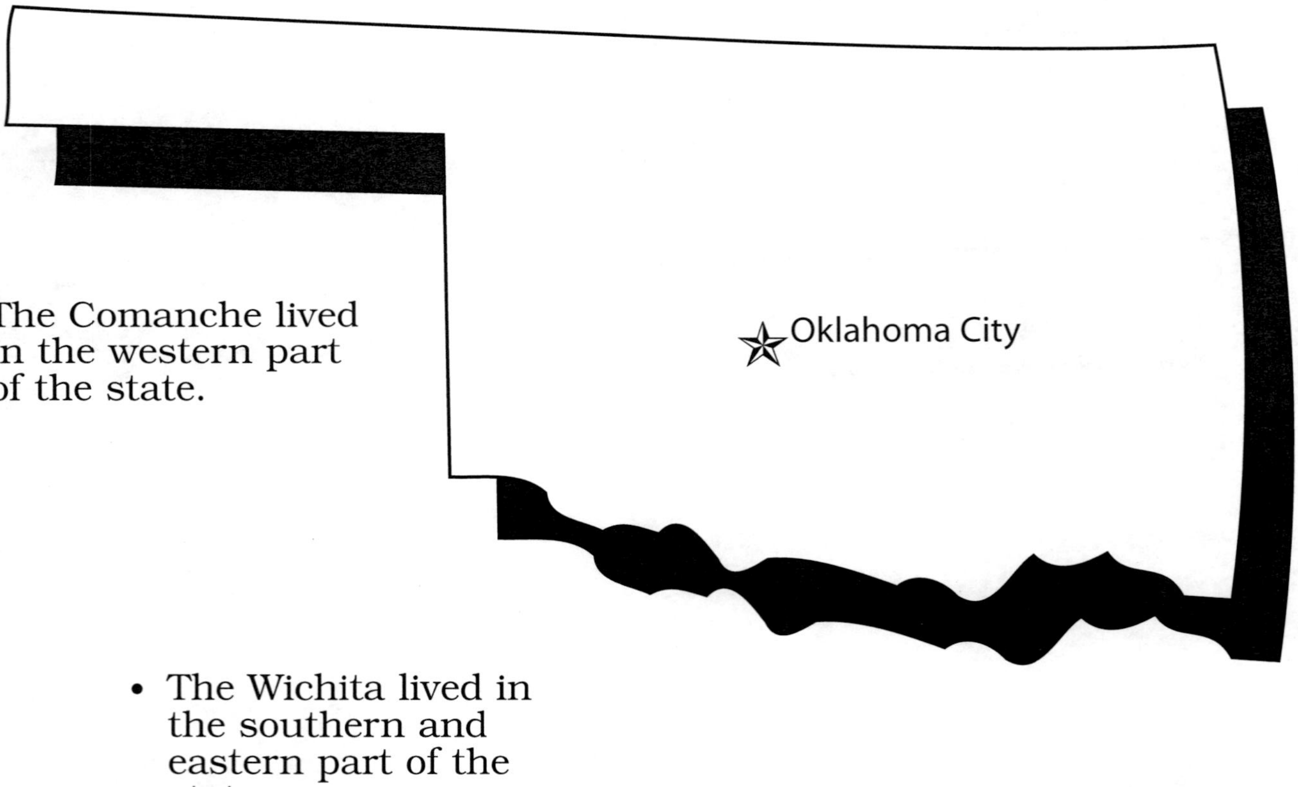

- The Comanche lived in the western part of the state.
- The Wichita lived in the southern and eastern part of the state.
- The Caddo and Pawnee lived in the eastern part of the state.

It's Money in the Bank!!

You spent the summer working as a reporter at *The Oklahoma Star*, and you made a lot of money...$500 to be exact! **Solve the math problems below using the information that is given.**

TOTAL EARNED: $500.00

I will pay back my Mom this much for money I borrowed when I first started working. Thanks, Mom! A. $20.00

subtract A from $500 B. __________

I will give my little brother this much money for taking my phone messages while I was at work: C. $10.00

subtract C from B D. __________

I will spend this much on a special treat or reward for myself: E. $25.00

subtract E from D F. __________

I will save this much for college: G. $300.00

subtract G from F H. __________

I will put this much in my new savings account so I can buy school clothes: I. $100.00

subtract I from H J. __________

TOTAL STILL AVAILABLE (use answer J) __________

TOTAL SPENT (add A, C, and E) __________

ANSWERS: B.$480 D.$470 F.$445 H.$145 J.$45 Total available: $45 Total spent: $55

Good Golly! Oklahoma Geography Word Search!

Find the names of these Oklahoma cities in the Word Search below:

ALVA
ANADARKO
BOISE CITY
EDMOND
ENID
GOODWELL
GUTHRIE
GUYMON
OKLAHOMA CITY
SHAWNEE
STILLWATER
TONKAWA
WEATHERFORD
WOODWARD

B O I S E C I T Y G I E N O D
K F G W L B J E N I D S A K G
G U Y M O N A G R H O L A L E
G O O D W E L L E A T U N A T
F W O O D W A R D L E N A H E
S T W E A T H E R F O R D O D
F M S H A W N E E U R P A M M
C D H L R A L V A B X K R A O
X L T O N K A W A K N R K C N
A K R V S T G H P X A K O I D
K H G U T H R I E Y L M S T G
D E S T I L L W A T E R X Y A

How Many People in Oklahoma?

STATE OF OKLAHOMA

CENSUS REPORT

Every ten years, it's time for Oklahomans to stand up and be counted. Since 1790, the United States has conducted a census, or count, of each of its citizens. **Practice filling out a pretend census form.**

Name ______________________________ Age ☐

Place of Birth ______________________________

Current Address ______________________________

Does your family own or rent where you live? ______________

How long have you lived in Oklahoma? ____________

How many people are in your family? ____________

How many females? ☐ How many males? ☐

What are their ages? ______________

How many rooms are in your house? ☐

How is your home heated? ______________

How many cars does your family own? ☐

How many telephones are in your home? ☐

Is your home a farm? __________

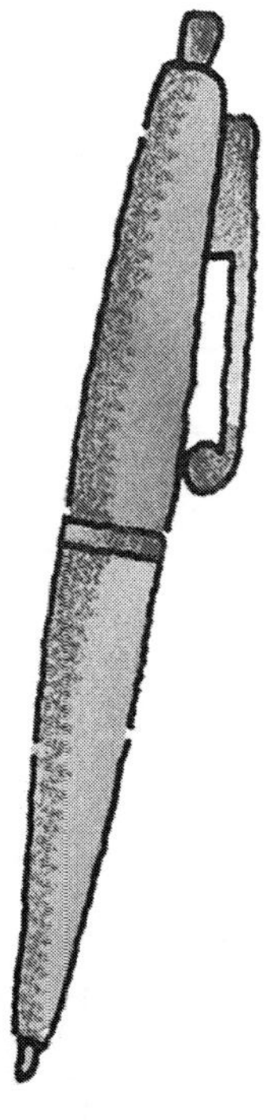

Sounds pretty nosy, doesn't it? But a census is very important. The information is used for all kinds of purposes, including setting budgets, zoning land, determining how many schools to build, and much more. The census helps Oklahoma leaders plan for the future needs of its citizens. Hey, that's you!!

Oklahoma Cities!

Circle Oklahoma City in red. It's the state capital.
Circle Anadarko in brown. Indian City is located there.
Circle Pawhuska in yellow. It's the capital of the Osage Indian Nation.
Circle Muskogee in green. It's where you can see the U.S.S. *Batfish* and Fort Gibson.
Circle Bartlesville in black. It's where the first commercial oil well was drilled in Oklahoma.

Add your city or town to the map if it's not here. Circle it in orange. Give it a ☺ symbol to show you live there.

Oops! The compass rose is missing its cardinal directions.

Write N, S, E, W, on the compass rose.

Endangered and Threatened Oklahoma!

Each state has a list of the endangered species in their state. An animal is labeled endangered when it is in danger of becoming extinct. Land development, changes in climate and weather, and changes in the number of predators are all factors that can cause an animal to become extinct. Today many states are passing laws to help save animals on the endangered species list.

Can you help rescue these endangered and threatened animals by filling in their names below?

1. I ___ D ___ ___ N ___ B ___ ___
2. O ___ A ___ K C ___ V ___ F ___ ___ H
3. B ___ ___ D E ___ G ___ ___
4. W ___ O ___ P ___ N ___ C ___ A ___ E
5. P ___ R ___ G ___ I ___ E F ___ L ___ ___ N
6. P ___ P ___ ___ G P ___ ___ V ___ ___

Circle the animal that is extinct (not here anymore).

ANSWERS: 1.Indiana bat 2.Ozark cavefish 3.bald eagle 4.whooping crane 5.peregrine falcon 6.piping plover

Sooners Sing Along to Oklahoma's State Song!

"Oklahoma" was written by Richard Rodgers and Oscar Hammerstein II as part of a musical play with the same name.

"Oklahoma" (first verse)

Brand new state! Brand new state, gonna treat you great!
Gonna give you barley, carrots, and pertaters,
Pasture fer the cattle, Spinach and Temayters!
Flowers on the prairie where the June bugs zoom,
Plen'y of air and plen'y of room,
Plen'y of room to swing a rope!
Plen'y of heart and plen'y of hope!

1. What does the first line of the song say that Oklahoma is?

____

2. What are two things it will give you?

____

3. What are two things there are plenty of?

____

4. What do you think the word "temayters" means?

____

5. What kind of bugs will zoom?

____

ANSWERS: 1.a brand new state 2.barley, carrots, pertaters/potatoes, pasture, spinach, temayters/tomatoes 3.air, room, heart, hope 4.tomatoes 5.June bugs

Getting Ready To Vote!

When you turn 18, you will be eligible to vote. Your vote counts! Many elections have been won by just a few votes. The following is a form for your personal voting information. You will need to do some research to get all the answers!

I will be eligible to vote on this date ________________

I live in this Congressional District ______________

I live in this State Senate District ________________

I live in this State Representative District __________

I live in this Voting Precinct _______________________

The first local election I can vote in will be _________

The first state election I can vote in will be _________

The first national election I can vote in will be ______

The governor of our state is _______________________

One of my state senators is ____

One of my state representatives is ____________________________________

The local public office I would like to run for is _______________________

The state public office I would like to run for is _______________________

The federal public office I would like to run for is _____________________

Oklahoma State Seal!

The state seal was developed from the history of the state. At the center of the seal is a five-pointed star with a circle inside it. In the circle are three figures, the Frontiersman, the Indian, and Justice. Above the figures is the state motto. In the upper-left point of the star is the symbol of the Cherokee Nation, and in the center point is the seal of the Chickasaw Nation. In the upper-right point is the symbol of the Choctaw nation, and in the lower-right point is the Seminole Nation's emblem. The lower-left point of the star shows the Creek Nation's symbol. There are 45 stars around the star to represent the states that were in the Union in 1907. The larger star in the center represents Oklahoma becoming the 46th state. **Color the state seal.**

Animal Scramble!

Unscramble the names of these animals you might find in your Oklahoma backyard.

Write the answers in the word wheel below the picture of each animal.

1. ***kipchnum*** Hint: She can store more than a hundred seeds in her cheeks!
2. ***ethiw-dleait ered*** Hint: He raises the underside of his tail to signal danger!
3. ***nrocoac*** Hint: He has very sensitive "fingers" and uses them to find food.
4. ***ntseare ttoncoliat bitbra*** Hint: She would love to eat the cabbages in your garden!
5. ***yarg lquiersr*** Hint: He scurries around all day, burying and digging up acorns!

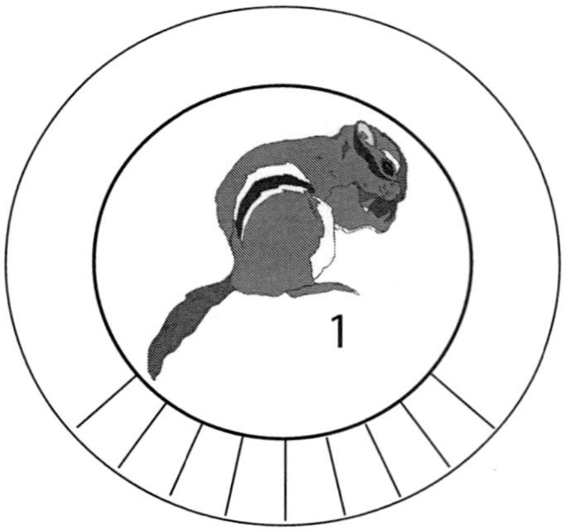

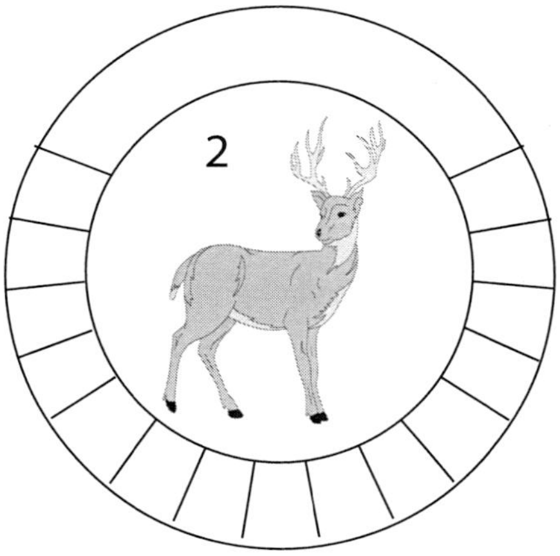

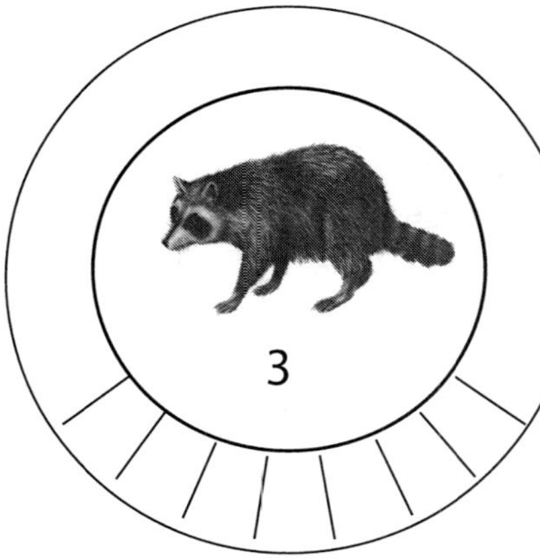

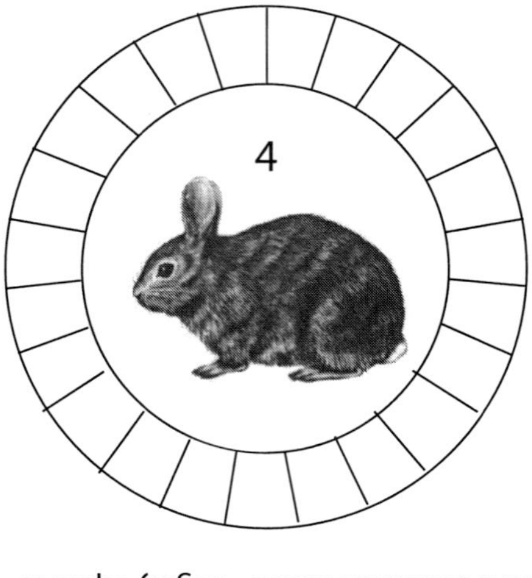

ANSWERS: 1. chipmunk 2. white–tailed deer 3. raccoon 4. eastern cottontail rabbit 5. gray squirrel

A Quilt Of Many Counties!

Oklahoma has 77 counties. Every city or town in Oklahoma belongs to a county.

- **Label your county. Color it red.**
- **Label the counties that touch your county. Color them blue.**
- **Now color the rest of the counties.**

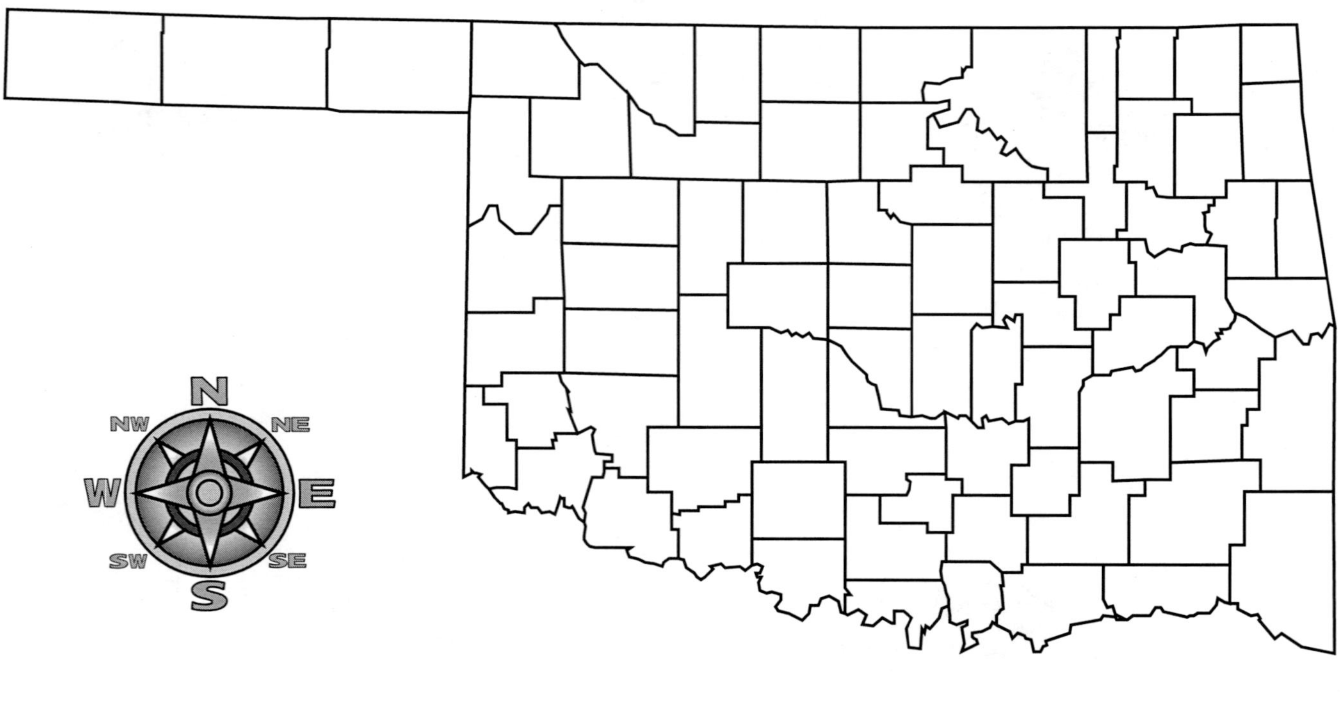

2 FOR 1

Sooner Sets!

2 FOR 1

How many of these two-name Oklahoma places can you match? You might need a map or an atlas to help you figure them out. For each "first half," write the letter of the "second half."

_____	1. Bethel	A. Wolf
_____	2. Boise	B. Springs
_____	3. Broken	C. Oak
_____	4. Burns	D. Chief
_____	5. Cleo	E. Bow
_____	6. El	F. Enid
_____	7. Fort	G. Flat
_____	8. Little	H. Park
_____	9. Lone	I. City
_____	10. Nicoma	J. Reno
_____	11. North	K. Acres
_____	12. Red	L. Cobb

ANSWERS: 1.K 2.I 3.E 4.G 5.B 6.J 7.L 8.D 9.A 10.H 11.F 12.C

Contributions by State Minorities!

Many African-Americans came to the region as cowboys, settlers, gunfighters, and farmers. They helped the Union win the Battle of Honey Springs, and were the Buffalo Soldiers who helped to keep the peace after the Civil War. By 1907, there were more African-Americans in Oklahoma than any other group.

When Congress passed the Indian Removal Act in 1830, the Five Civilized Tribes were moved into eastern Oklahoma, called the Indian Territory. After the Civil War many of the Indians were moved again onto reservations. Today, 35 tribes maintain tribal councils in Oklahoma.

Many African-Americans and Native Americans have made, and continue to make, significant contributions to the state of Oklahoma. Below are a few.

Try matching each person with his/her accomplishments.

_____1. William Wayne Keeler

_____ 2. Ralph Ellison

_____ 3. Jim Thorpe

_____ 4. Sequoyah (George Gist)

_____ 5. C.L. Cooper

_____ 6. Sydney Lyons

_____ 7. Leona Mitchell

_____ 8. John Hope Franklin

A. wrote several books on the history of blacks in America

B. created an alphabet for the Cherokee language

C. African-American essayist and novelist, won the National Book Award in 1953

D. only black physician in Eufaula from 1908 to the 1930s

E. developed the East India Toilet Goods Company after moving to Oklahoma in 1905

F. opera singer who performed with the New York City Metropolitan Opera Company

G Chief of the Cherokee Nation in 1949, CEO of Phillips Petroleum Company in 1967

H. won two gold medals in the 1912 Olympics

ANSWERS: 1.G 2.C 3.H 4.B 5.D 6.E 7.F 8.A

Let's Make Words!

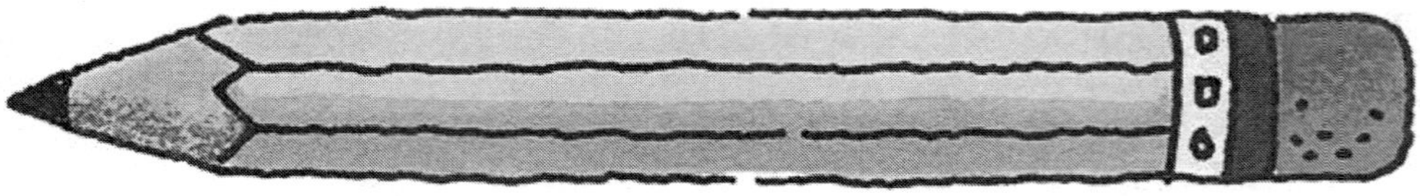

Make up as many words as you can from Oklahoma's state motto:

"Labor Conquers All Things!"

Wild Things!

The Oklahoma City Zoo is the oldest zoo in the Southwest! It was established in 1904, covers more than 110 acres (44 hectares) of land, and is the home of almost 2,000 animals. Almost 500 species of animals live at the Zoo. You can visit habitats where reptiles, amphibians, big cats, apes, and many other animals live! The Zoo is a living museum, and has a beautiful botanical garden.

Name these animals you might find at the zoo.

1. ___ ___ ___ ___ ___

2. ___ ___ ___ ___ ___

3. ___ ___ ___ ___ ___ ___

4. ___ ___ ___ ___ ___

5. ___ ___ ___ ___

6. ___ ___ ___ ___ ___ ___ ___ ___

7. ___ ___ ___ ___ ___ ___ ___ ___ ___

ANSWERS: 1.tiger 2.snake 3.monkey 4.camel 5.lion 6.elephant 7.alligator

Which Founding Person Am I?

From the Word Bank, find my name and fill in the blank.

WORD BANK

William Bennett Bizzell | Zebulon Pike

Owen K. Garriott | Maria Tallchief

Auguste Pierre Chouteau

1. I was a fur trader and a pioneer. I founded the first permanent European settlement in Oklahoma in 1796.

   WHO AM I? ______________ ____________ ___________________

2. I was a soldier and explorer, told to follow the Arkansas River to its source. I tried unsuccessfully to climb a mountain that is now named for me.

   WHO AM I? ________________________ ______________________

3. I was the first president of the University of Oklahoma. I also helped to set up the University of Oklahoma Press.

   WHO AM I? _______________ ____________ ___________________

4. I was a ballerina from Fairfax. I founded the Chicago City Ballet.

   WHO AM I? _____________________ _________________________

5. I was an astronaut from Enid. I was part of the Skylab space project.

   WHO AM I? _________________ ____ ______________________

ANSWERS: 1.Auguste Pierre Chouteau 2.Zebulon Pike 3.William Bennett Bizzell 4.Maria Tallchief 5.Owen K. Garriott

It Could Happen– And It Did!

These historical events from Oklahoma's past are all out of order.

Can you put them back together in the correct order? (There's a great big hint at the end of each sentence.)

- The McClellan-Kerr Arkansas River Navigation System opens (1971)
- David L. Payne organizes the "Boomers" (1879)
- Spain gives the area including Oklahoma back to France (1800)
- French fur trader Juchereau de St. Denis sails up the Red River, and is the first Frenchman to see Oklahoma (1714)
- The Land Run begins (1889)
- Oklahoma's capital moves from Guthrie to Oklahoma City (1910)
- Apache chief Geronimo is imprisoned at Fort Sill (1894)
- The first commercial coal mine opens in Oklahoma (1872)
- George Sibley's expedition crosses the Great Salt Plains (1811)
- Oklahomans impeach Governor John C. Walton for abuse of power (1923)

1. ______________________________
2. ______________________________
3. ______________________________
4. ______________________________
5. ______________________________
6. ______________________________
7. ______________________________
8. ______________________________
9. ______________________________
10. ______________________________

Make a Buffalo Skin Vest!

Native Americans wore clothing that was made from the skins of buffalo or deer. To make your buffalo skin vest, you will need a brown paper bag. Lay the bag flat, as shown in the picture. Cut out holes for your arms and neck. Make a long slit in one side of the bag.

Ideas for decorating your vest:

- glue buttons, glitter, and feathers on the vest
- use markers or crayons to draw Native American symbols on the vest
- make fringe at the bottom of the bag by snipping along the edges of the bag
- decorate your vest with beads, shells, etc.

Get together with your friends and have a great "pow-wow"!

Oklahoma People!

A state is not just towns and mountains and rivers. A state is its people! But the really important people in a state are not always famous. You may know them—they may be your mom, your dad, or your teacher. The average, everyday person is the one who helps to make the state a good state. How? By working hard, by paying taxes, by voting, and by helping Oklahoma children grow up to be good state citizens!

Match each Oklahoma person with his/her accomplishment.

1. William L. Couch
2. William Wrigley
3. Orlando B. Swain
4. Henry Bellmon
5. Robert M. Jones
6. Cora V. Diehl
7. Milly Francis
8. J. H. "Jake" Bartles

A. "Oklahoma's Pocahontas," first woman awarded a Congressional Medal

B. first woman elected to a public office in Oklahoma

C. manufactured his first package of chewing gum in Guthrie

D. first millionaire in the Choctaw Nation

E. established the first flour mill in Indian Territory in 1877

F. Oklahoma's first Republican governor

G. first mayor of Oklahoma City

H. created the Creek Indian Memorial Association in 1923

ANSWERS: 1.G 2.C 3.H 4.F 5.D 6.B 7.A 8.E

Similar Sooner Symbols!

Oklahoma has many symbols including a state bird, tree, seal, and flag. **Circle the item in each row that is *not* a symbol of Oklahoma.**

I Want To Be A Cowboy!

Oklahoma is the land not only of Indians, but of cowboys, too. After the Civil War, Texas ranchers raised a lot of beef cattle, but had nowhere to sell it. They knew that people on the East Coast would buy the beef, but they had to get the cattle to the railroads. Unfortunately, at the time the closest ones were in Kansas!

Oklahoma was between Texas and Kansas, and so between 1866 and 1889, the cowboys blazed cattle trails across the territory. As the cowboys drove their cattle across the area, they also noticed that it was terrific grazing land! Many cattle ranches were built all through the area, and it still is a busy livestock center today.

Look at the map of Oklahoma below. "Blaze" a trail or two for a cowboy to take his cattle from Texas to Kansas. Remember that it's hard to get cattle to go up mountains, or across big rivers.

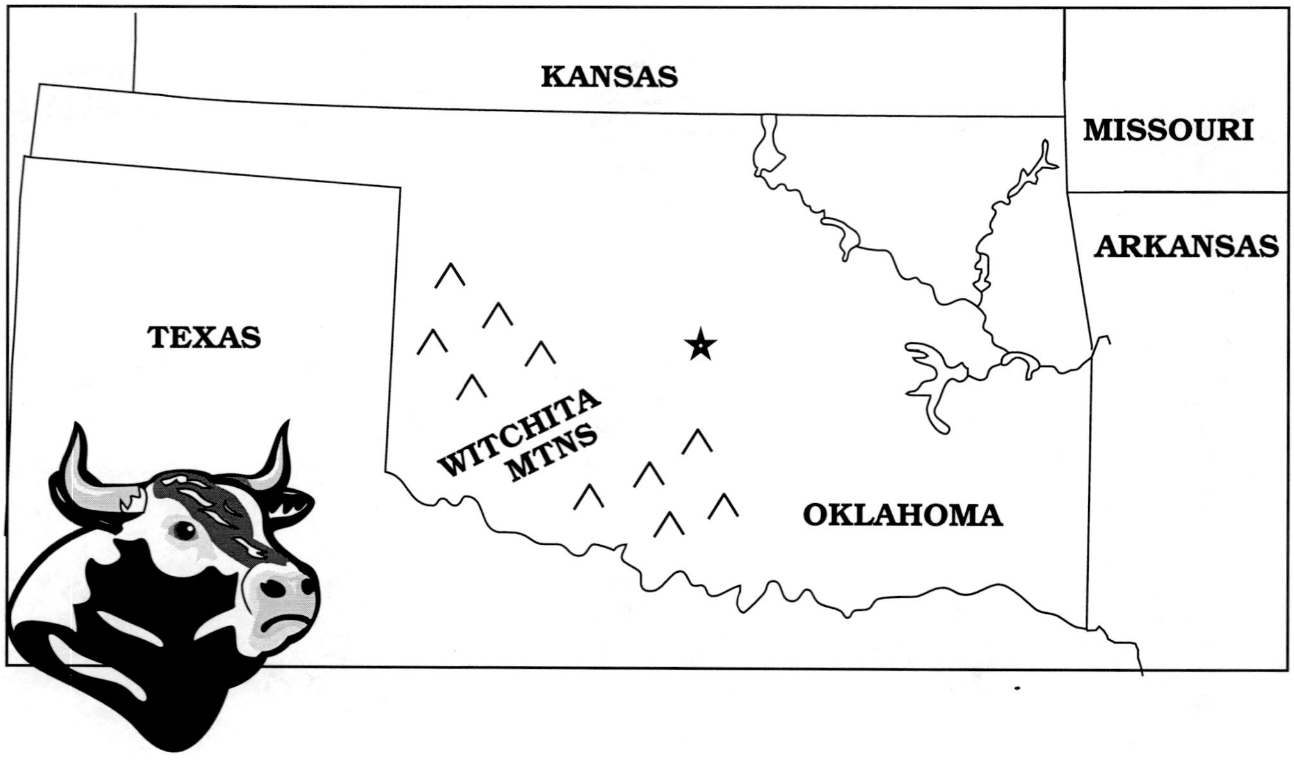

Oklahoma Settlements Word Wheel!

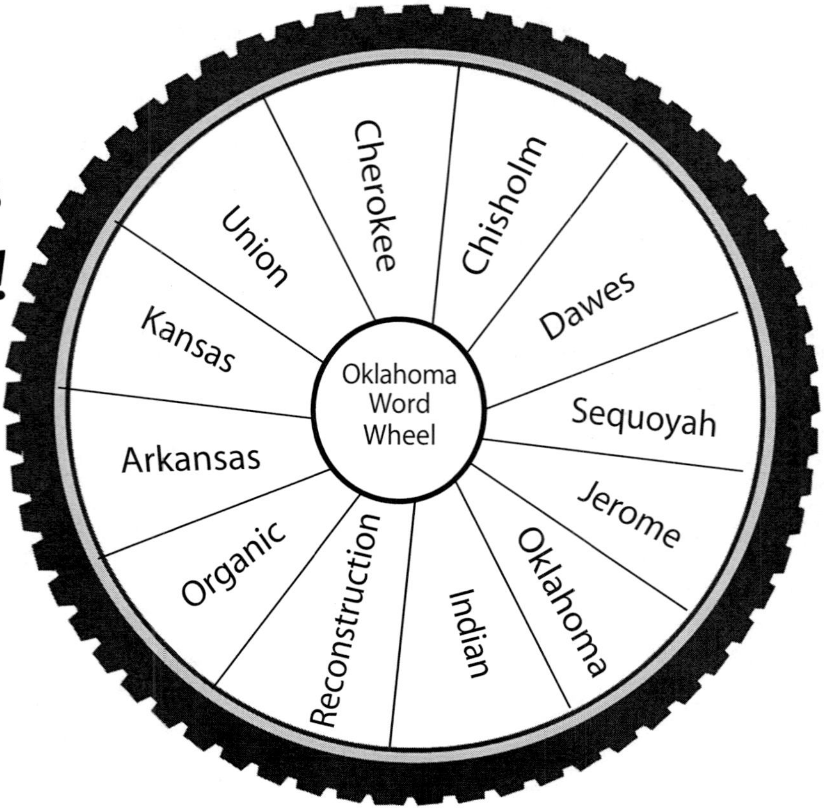

Spin the Word Wheel of Oklahoma names to complete the sentences below.

1. From 1819 to 1824, Oklahoma was part of the __________________ Territory.
2. From 1824 to 1907, the eastern part of Oklahoma was called __________________ Territory.
3. The western part of Oklahoma was part of the __________________ Territory between 1890 and 1907.
4. The Oklahoma __________________ Act of 1890 took half of the Indian Territory and made it into the Oklahoma Territory.
5. In 1893, 6 million acres (2.4 million hectares) of the __________________ Outlet were opened for settlement.
6. In 1900, the __________________ Commission was appointed to negotiate for the land belonging to the Plains Indians.
7. One of the best-known cattle trails across Oklahoma was the ____________________ Trail.
8. In 1887, the ____________________ Commission was appointed to acquire the land owned by the Five Civilized Tribes.
9. After the Civil War, the Five Civilized Tribes had to sign ____________________ Treaties that made them give up some of their land in Indian Territory.
10. Right before the beginning of the 1889 Land Run, people assembled on Oklahoma's borders with Arkansas and ____________________ .

ANSWERS: 1.Arkansas 2.Indian 3.Oklahoma 4.Organic 5.Cherokee 6.Jerome 7.Chisholm 8.Dawes 9.Reconstruction 10.Kansas

Know your Oklahoma Facts!

Pop quiz! It's time to test your knowledge of Oklahoma! Try to answer all of the questions before you look at the answers.

1. The capital of Oklahoma is...
   a. Tulsa
   b. Norman
   c. Oklahoma City
   d. Boise City

2. Oklahoma's state animal is the...
   a. Buffalo
   b. White-tailed Deer
   c. Scissor-tailed Flycatcher
   d. Horse

3. Oklahoma became a state in...
   a. 1997
   b. 1807
   c. 1897
   d. 1907

4. Oklahoma's name comes from an Indian word meaning...
   a. "land of rivers"
   b. "red people"
   c. "green people"
   d. "prairie"

5. Which of these was NOT one of the Five Civilized Tribes?
   a. Choctaw
   b. Cherokee
   c. Shawnee
   d. Creek

6. Oklahoma's state rock is...
   a. Galena
   b. Quartz
   c. Barite Rose Rock
   d. Greenstone

7. The Oklahoma Organic Act turned which half of Indian Territory into Oklahoma Territory?
   a. north
   b. west
   c. south
   d. east

8. The Buffalo Soldiers were...
   a. African-Americans
   b. Native Americans
   c. Hispanic Americans
   d. Buffalo

9. The first newspaper published in Oklahoma was the...
   a. *Choctaw Intelligencer*
   b. *Cherokee Advocate*
   c. *Oklahoma Star*
   d. *Choctaw Telegraph*

10. Oklahoma's state motto is...
   a. United we stand, divided we fall
   b. All for one, one for all
   c. Labor conquers all things
   d. To be, rather than to seem

ANSWERS: 1.c 2.a 3.d 4.b 5.c 6.c 7.b 8.a 9.b 10.c

Sooner Scavenger Hunt!

This is a fun hunt that includes your friends or classmates. Read the list below, find someone who has "been there and done that," get their signature and move on to the next item on your list. See how fast you can complete the scavenger hunt. Write down the answers to part 2, and have your teacher, or parent, check them.

Part 1
Find someone who has:

- been to the state capitol building ______________________
- seen an Oklahoma Sooners game ______________________
- met a cowboy ______________________
- visited the Cherokee National Museum ______________________
- attended a rodeo ______________________
- been to Fort Sill ______________________
- seen a twister ______________________

Part 2
Find somone who can:

- tell you Oklahoma's statehood date ______________________
- say the state motto ______________________
- name the state capital ______________________
- tell who Sequoyah was ______________________
- name a major Oklahoma river ______________________
- name the governor of Oklahoma ______________________
- name the state tree ______________________

Oklahoma Origins!

Oklahoma has a rich Native American heritage. You can see this in many of the place names around the state.

See if you can match these names with their meanings in the original Native American languages.

_____	1. Oklahoma	A. iron road (Choctaw)
_____	2. Pocola	B. barking waters (Seminole)
_____	3. Oologah	C. red people (Choctaw)
_____	4. Talihina	D. chief (Creek)
_____	5. Catoosa	E. ten miles from town (Choctaw)
_____	6. Wewoka	F. on the hill (Cherokee)
_____	7. Wetumka	G. noisy or sounding waters (Creek)
_____	8. Migco	H. dark cloud (Cherokee)

ANSWERS: 1.C 2.E 3.H 4.A 5.F 6.B 7.G 8.D

Terrific Tallgrass Prairie Preserve!

North of Pawhuska, you can find a 37,000 acre (14,973 hectare) area that is populated with buffalo, deer, bobcats, badgers, and many other creatures. Tallgrass Prairie Preserve has been run by the Nature Conservancy since 1989. It's intended to restore part of the prairie landscape to the way it was before the settlers arrived. In 1993, a herd of 300 buffalo was introduced into the area, and is expected to grow to 2,000 animals before too long!

A *haiku* is a three line poem with a certain number of syllables in each line. Look at the example below:

The first line has 5 syllables	Oh, Tall/grass Prair/ie 1 2 3 4 5
The second line has 7 syllables	Buf/fa/lo, deer, and oth/ers 1 2 3 4 5 6 7
The third line has 5 syllables	Live in har/mon/y! 1 2 3 4 5

Now, write your own h*aiku* about the beautiful Tallgrass Prairie.

____

____

____

Take Refuge!

Oklahoma has made a real effort to preserve many of the natural habitats around the state. There are 52 state parks and recreation areas, and some have historical sites. There are also national forests and wildlife refuges. Each is designed to help preserve certain types of animals, plants, and environments.

Unscramble the names of these Oklahoma refuges, forests, and parks.

1. H A U Q O Y E S ___ ___ ___ ___ ___ ___ ___ ___ State Park

2. M T O I O S G N I H ___ ___ ___ ___ ___ ___ ___ ___ ___ ___ National Wildlife Refuge

3. A A C H T I O U ___ ___ ___ ___ ___ ___ ___ ___ National Forest

4. E E O R H C E K N D I L A G N ___ ___ ___ ___ ___ ___ ___ ___ ___ ___ ___ ___ ___ ___ ___ State Park

5. Z T U Q R A N T I A N O U M ___ ___ ___ ___ ___ ___ ___ ___ ___ ___ ___ ___ ___ ___ State Park

6. C K L A B T E T L K E ___ ___ ___ ___ ___ ___ ___ ___ ___ ___ ___ National Grassland

ANSWERS: 1.Sequoyah 2.Tishomingo 3.Ouachita 4.Cherokee Landing 5.Quartz Mountain 6.Black Kettle

Sizing Up the Sooner State!

Oklahoma is the 20th largest state in the U.S. It has an area of 69,903 square miles (181,048 square kilometers).

Can you answer the following questions?

1. How many states are there in the United States?

____

2. This many states are smaller than our state:

____

3. This many states are larger than our state:

____

4. One mile = 5,280 ____ ____ ____ ____

HINT: 

5. Draw a "square foot" here:

ANSWERS: 1.50 2.30 3.19 4.feet 5.

Alabaster Caverns

Northwestern Oklahoma is the home of one of nature's incredible wonders. About 30 miles (48 kilometers) north of Woodward, you will find the Alabaster Caverns State Park. Alabaster Cave was formed about 250 million years ago by water forming tunnels in the gypsum, dolomite, and shale deposits in the area. It's the largest public gypsum cave in the country. The huge underground cavern is filled with multicolored alabaster and selenite crystals, and the main cavern has been lighted to show off the brilliant colors. Alabaster is a type of gypsum that can be carved into ornaments, and selenite is gypsum crystals. It's a truly beautiful sight!

Pretend that you are a "spelunker" (person who explores caves). What sort of tools do you think you'd need to thoroughly investigate a cave? Circle the tools you'd need below.

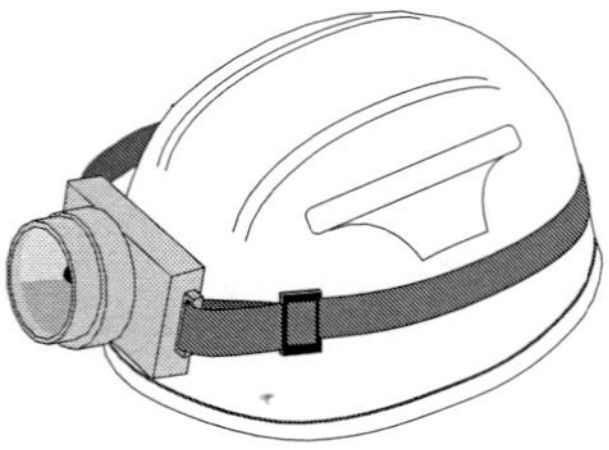

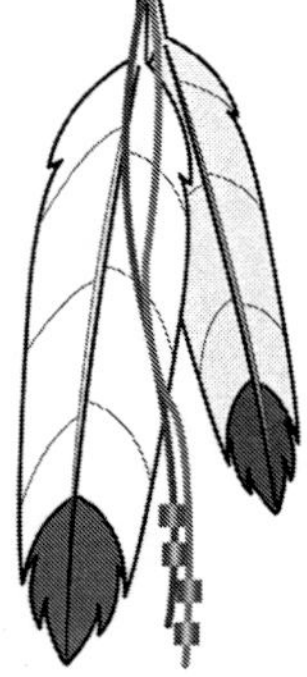